WOMEN IN HISTORY

Women of the Renaissance

Melissa Thomson and Ruth Dean

LUCENT BOOKS

An imprint of Thomson Gale, a part of The Thomson Corporation

THOMSON

GALE

Detroit • New York • San Francisco • San Diego • New Haven, Conn. • Waterville, Maine • London • Munich

For more information, contact
Lucent Books
27500 Drake Rd.
Farmington Hills, MI 48331-3535
Or you can visit our Internet site at http://www.gale.com

LIBRARY OF CONGRESS CATALOGING-IN-PUBLICATION DATA

Thomson, Melissa.
  Women of the Renaissance / by Melissa Thomson and Ruth Dean.
    p. cm. — (Women in history)
  Includes bibliographical references and index.
  ISBN 1-59018-473-4 (hard cover : alk. paper)
  1. Women—History—Renaissance, 1450–1600—Juvenile literature. 2. Renaissance—Juvenile literature. I. Dean, Ruth, 1947– II. Title. III. Series: Women in history (San Diego, Calif.)
  HQ1148.T46 2004
  305.4'09—dc22
 	
                                                          2004010849

Printed in the United States of America

Contents

Foreword

The story of the past as told in traditional historical writings all too often leaves the impression that if men are not the only actors in the narrative, they are assuredly the main characters. With a few notable exceptions, males were the political, military, and economic leaders in virtually every culture throughout recorded time. Since traditional historical scholarship focuses on the public arenas of government, foreign relations, and commerce, the actions and ideas of men—or at least of powerful men—are naturally at the center of conventional accounts of the past.

In the last several decades, however, many historians have abandoned their predecessors' emphasis on "great men" to explore the past "from the bottom up," a phenomenon that has had important consequences for the study of women's history. These social historians, as they are known, focus on the day-to-day experiences of the "silent majority"—those people typically omitted from conventional scholarship because they held relatively little political or economic sway within their societies. In the new social history, members of ethnic and racial minorities, factory workers, peasants, slaves, children, and women are no longer relegated to the background but are placed at the very heart of the narrative.

Around the same time social historians began broadening their research to include women and other previously neglected elements of society, the feminist movement of the late 1960s and 1970s was also bringing unprecedented attention to the female heritage. Feminists hoped that by examining women's past experiences, contemporary women could better understand why and how gender-based expectations had developed in their societies, as well as how they might reshape inherited—and typically restrictive—economic, social, and political roles in the future.

Today, some four decades after the feminist and social history movements gave new impetus to the study of women's history, there is a rich and continually growing body of work on all aspects of women's lives in the past. The Lucent Books Women in History series draws upon this abundant and diverse literature to introduce students to women's experiences within a variety of past cultures and time periods in terms of the distinct roles they filled. In their capacities as workers, activists, and artists, women exerted significant influence on important events whether they conformed to or broke from traditional roles. The Women in History titles depict extraordinary women who managed to attain positions of influence in their male-dominated societies, including such celebrated heroines as the feisty medieval queen Eleanor of Aquitaine, the brilliant propagandist of the American Revolution Mercy Otis Warren, and the courageous African American activist of the Civil War era Harriet Tubman. Included as well are the stories of the ordinary—and often overlooked—women of the past who also helped shape their societies' myriad ways—moral, intellectual, and economic—without straying far from customary gender roles: the housewives and mothers, schoolteachers and church volunteers, midwives and nurses and wartime camp followers.

In this series, readers will discover that many of these unsung women took more significant parts in the great political and social upheavals of their day than has often been recognized. In *Women of the American Revolution,* for example, students will learn how American housewives assumed a crucial role in helping the Patriots win the war against Britain. They accomplished this by planting and harvesting fields, producing and trading goods, and doing whatever else was necessary to maintain the family farm or business in the absence of their soldier husbands despite the heavy burden of housekeeping and child-care duties they already bore. By their self-sacrificing actions, competence, and ingenuity, these anonymous heroines not only kept their families alive, but kept the economy of their struggling young nation going as well during eight long years of war.

Each volume in this series contains generous commentary from the works of respected contemporary scholars, but the Women in History series particularly emphasizes quotations from primary sources such as diaries, letters, and journals whenever possible to allow the women of the past to speak for themselves. These firsthand accounts not only help students to better understand the dimensions of women's daily spheres—the work they did, the organizations they belonged to, the physical hardships they faced—but also how they viewed themselves and their actions in the light of their society's expectations for their sex.

The distinguished American historian Mary Beard once wrote that women have always been a "force in history." It is hoped that the books in this series will help students to better appreciate the vital yet often little-known ways in which women of the past have shaped their societies and cultures.

Introduction:
The Renaissance Woman

The Renaissance, which began in Italy in the fourteenth century, was a time of dynamic change in European society sparked by a renewed interest in ancient Greek and Roman art and learning. Fueled by economic growth, this intellectual rebirth led to changes and advances in education, exploration, religion, science, art, literature, and architecture that spread across Europe into England and lasted into the seventeenth century. This was the age of Leonardo da Vinci, Michelangelo, Christopher Columbus, William Shakespeare, and Queen Elizabeth I of England. The Renaissance influenced the lives of both men and women, but in markedly different ways, with far fewer women than men achieving the highest levels of power and status. Cultural institutions and social roles limited women's active participation in the world around them.

Few women took part in the new intellectual movement called humanism, which centered on human capabilities rather than on the divine ordering of society that medieval people perceived. Humanists emphasized the dignity and worth of the individual and valued education because it allowed people to develop skills that would contribute to society. Not all skills were deemed suitable for all people, however. Renaissance noblemen—but rarely noblewomen—were encouraged to learn foreign languages, oratory, horsemanship, and the art of war so that they could serve their king and country. For women, however, gaining an education remained the privilege of a very few.

Christianity remained the most powerful institution in European society, and though it too was changed by new and rapidly spreading ways of thinking, its strictures on women's proper sphere and status were not much loosened. One of the greatest changes that shook the European world was the late Renaissance religious movement known as the Reformation, led by men and women who aimed to "reform" the Church of Rome because they saw it as extravagant and corrupt. Some strove to reform the church from within, while others broke away to form new religious institutions. They became known as Protestants because of their "protest" against what they disliked in the Roman Church. Religious disagreements resulted in discrimination, persecution, and war, and affected women at every level of society.

To understand the significant roles women *did* play during the Renaissance, it helps to understand the general status of women in Renaissance society.

Renaissance Social Structure

Although political structures varied across Europe, the social structure everywhere fell into roughly three levels. At the top was the upper class, consisting of the

This detail from Renaissance master Raphael's painting The School of Athens *depicts the ancient Greek mathematician Euclid explaining a point of geometry.*

Italy: Birthplace of the Renaissance

THE ALPS

MONTFERRAT

DUCHY OF MILAN

MANTUA

SAVOY

Turin

Milan

REPUBLIC OF VENICE

Mantua

Parma

Padua

Venice

Genoa

PARMA

Modena

REPUBLIC OF GENOA

FIVIZANNO

MASSA

LUCCA

Pisa

MODENA

San Marino

Florence

Adriatic Sea

TUSCANY

PAPAL STATES

PIOMBINO

Rome

SARDINIA

Tyrrhenian Sea

NAPLES

Naples

The Grand Canal

The Duomo

St. Peter's Basilica

Mediterranean Sea

N

wealthiest, most educated members of society. In monarchies the upper class included the royal family and other high-ranking families known as the nobility, or aristocracy. Below them was the middle class, a group that grew markedly during the Renaissance and that consisted of merchants, traders, craftsmen, farmers, and others who were relatively prosperous. At the bottom of society were the lower-class, poor workers who comprised about three-quarters of the entire population and whose lives were a nearly constant struggle for food and other basic necessities. Within any class, women ranked lower than men, girls lower than boys.

All women, regardless of class, were strongly affected by the sweeping changes in living conditions that transformed Europe in the Renaissance era. The outbreaks of plague that had swept Europe during the Middle Ages diminished in the fifteenth and sixteenth centuries, leading to growth and shifts in population. In 1400 Europe's population numbered around 45 million; by 1600 it had risen to 89 million. Increasingly, people moved from rural farms to the towns, seeking work, and cities grew in size and importance, becoming economic centers. Skilled craftspeople—who were overwhelmingly male—produced goods that enterprising merchants sold across Europe, backed by a growing banking sector. Explorers using advanced navigational instruments and maps circled the globe, searching for and often bringing back gold, silver, spices, and raw materials that fueled economic growth.

The urban middle class profited most from economic development; as prices and profits rose throughout much of the sixteenth century, workers and peasants suffered. In general, women in both urban and rural settings remained economically disadvantaged, much as they were in the Middle Ages, since they earned only one-half to two-thirds the wages of men. Social and legal restrictions also challenged women and limited their ability to support themselves and their children.

Birth, Life, and Death

Despite scientific progress and advances in knowledge of human anatomy and the circulatory system, Renaissance medicine remained primitive. Little was known about hygiene or the causes of disease. Women's health was particularly precarious because many Renaissance wives spent most of their adult life pregnant or nursing a child. Repeated pregnancies were themselves a severe strain on a woman's body, and death from complications of childbirth was not unusual. Even the best available care could not guarantee a mother's survival. Despite her position of privilege, Jane Seymour, third wife of King Henry VIII of England, died within weeks of giving birth. The death rate for babies and children was also high, and it was not

Renaissance women, like the woman in this portrait by Raphael, spent most of their lives pregnant or nursing.

have married in their late teens, most boys in their early twenties.

Negative Views of Women

Despite their regional and religious differences, Renaissance Europeans held a uniform expectation of women: that they should be chaste, silent, and obedient. This strongly held and often-repeated requirement stemmed from the Renaissance focus on the biblical story of the Fall: the expulsion of the first man and woman, Adam and Eve, from paradise. In Renaissance advice books and other materials written by men to women (even books on gardening), Eve is frequently referred to as "your Grandmother Eve," reinforcing the idea that Eve passed down to all women her ability to tempt men (in handing Adam the forbidden fruit); her disobedience (in disobeying God's prohibition against eating fruit from the Tree of the Knowledge of Good and Evil); and her untrustworthy words (in telling Adam to eat the fruit). Renaissance men feared these qualities, which they saw in all women, and therefore constantly commanded women to be chaste, silent, and obedient.

This cultural fear of the powers of women led to the European witch-hunts, a widespread persecution that affected one community after another over a period of three centuries. From 1450 to 1750, church and political leaders put supposed "witch-

unusual for a Renaissance woman to lose most of her children to disease and accidents before they reached adulthood.

Average life expectancy for a Renaissance man or woman changed little from medieval times. A person reaching the age of twenty could expect to live to about age fifty. Although accurate records are scarce, it is evident that some Renaissance women who survived their childbearing years lived to age sixty or older. The legal age of marriage was twelve for girls and fourteen for boys, but most girls seem to es" on trial, and an estimated one hundred thousand people were convicted and executed, usually by being burned at the stake. Between 80 and 90 percent of these were women. Women were accused of flying on their broomsticks at night to join in huge assemblies where they made pacts with the devil and ate babies. Especially in the early years of the witch-hunts, the accused were poor old women who begged for food from

Pictured in this detail of Sandro Botticelli's Primavera *are the three Graces, the sister goddesses of Greek mythology who are the givers of charm and beauty.*

door to door, perhaps threatening to put a "spell" on the household if they were refused. As the panic swept through Europe, accused witches were tortured until they gave the names of others. In some villages, all but one or two of the women were put to death.

Women's Roles: Subordinate but Vital

The witchcraft persecutions were just one result of the fact that almost everywhere in Europe women had no legal status. They could rarely own property or run a business. Their wages were often paid to their husbands or fathers, and they had no ability to enter into a legal contract. A woman rarely had the opportunity to choose her own husband, and she was generally trans-ferred from her father's household to her husband's as an item of property. Where widows were entitled to inherit their husbands' property, however, these women sometimes achieved a measure of independence.

While these cultural conditions placed women in a subordinate role, nonetheless, women played a vital part in the life of Renaissance Europe. Women of all classes worked hard to run their households and provide for their families. They bore and raised children, provided medical care and charitable support, and produced works of art. Within their assigned roles or by breaking cultural boundaries, women played important parts in the economic, political, religious, and cultural worlds of the Renaissance.

Chapter 1:
Wives, Mothers, and Caregivers

Great social and religious changes occurred during the Renaissance, leading to the development of new cultural expectations for women: They were now seen, above all, in the related roles of wife, mother, and caregiver. Of course women had married and given birth to children in earlier eras, and women were traditionally the primary caregivers in their communities. The difference was that Renaissance people believed the role of wife was the ideal role for a woman, and the most noble and fulfilling way she could live. Both religious and political leaders encouraged women to live up to this idealized image, to be a Good Wife. As Good Wives, women received respect, but they also experienced limitations on their ability to gain an education, voice an opinion, make decisions, earn a living, exert political power, and participate in Renaissance cultural life.

The Business of Housewifery

The role of Good Wife placed many responsibilities on a woman's shoulders, regardless of her social class. The life of a poor wife was probably the most difficult; she had to work during all of her waking hours to feed and clothe her family. As Renaissance writer Wye Saltonstall wrote, her life "is nothing but a continual stirring about business and housewifery, till she be laid in her grave, and then she rests from her labor."[1]

A wife of higher social standing did not do as much work with her own hands, but she constantly had to supervise the labor of her servants. To do this effectively, she needed to understand every step involved in the challenging tasks of brewing, cooking, baking, producing cloth and clothing, growing food, raising farm animals, making medicines, and caring for people who were sick or injured. The household account book of one English wife, Sarah Fell, shows that she was "active in planning kitchen gardens, making and caring for her own clothing and that of her children, and overseeing the production or purchase and care of household goods. She also supervised the dairy."[2]

A German booklet of the era, "Mirror of a Christian and Peaceful Household," further describes this role:

The wife is to discipline the children, take diligent care of the household, stay at home, keep her husband's secrets, be patient with his faults, and preserve her honor. The husband should instruct the children and servants to obey her, work hard to support the household, stay home at night, and give no cause for jealousy. [3]

Maintaining the Family

The responsibilities of the Renaissance Good Wife did not end with housekeeping tasks. Many women also educated their children and servants (who often joined a household as children). In addition, because men of this era were often forced to leave home for months or years to fight in a war, to serve at a king's court, or to help govern a region or kingdom, upper-class wives had to manage and defend the family's farms and castles when their husbands were away. In their husbands' absence, women assuming the role of host were expected

Rare Receipts for Cookery

Hannah Woolley worked as a servant in the household of Lady Mary Wroth before marrying Jeremy Woolley, a schoolteacher. In 1664 Hannah wrote *The Cooks Guide: or Rare Receipts for Cookery,* dedicating it "to all ladies and gentlewomen in general who love the art of preserving and cookery." Among the recipes in Woolley's cookbook are apricot pudding, candied spices, dressed sheep's foot, French bread, and oyster pie.

Woolley's recipe for hedgehog pudding is not made of hedgehog—it is bread pudding cooked in a rounded shape and then stuck with slivers of almonds. These made the cooked pudding look like a hedgehog, a small European animal with spines on its back that curls itself into a ball when frightened.

To make a hedgehog pudding
Take a twopenny loaf with fair water and a little milk, the yolks of five eggs and three whites, one grated nutmeg and a little salt, some sugar and a little rosewater. Then butter a wooden dish and put it in. Tie it up closely in a cloth that no water get in. Put it into boiling water, and when it is boiled slip it out into a dish and prick it full of blanched almonds cut in long slender pieces, and raisins of the sun cut in like manner. Pour on it rosewater, butter and sugar.

Women of the Renaissance

to offer formal hospitality to relatives, neighbors, and important people who were traveling nearby. Through such gestures, the wife safeguarded the family's physical well-being and property, and also its social standing and connections. Biographer Vita Sackville-West describes one such Renaissance wife, Anne Clifford, countess of Pembroke:

> She was born to rule over houses and households, to tyrannize over her dependents, to have an enormous number of grandchildren and great grandchildren . . . to fuss over their alliances, to give advice—and woe betide those who did not take it—to govern from the midst of a little court of her own, and to receive the homage of those who were summoned to visit her. [4]

"Let the Husband Give the Orders"

In the role of Good Wife, or preparing for it, most Renaissance women spent their lives under the rule of a man, first their father and then their husband. Lower-class girls did not always go straight from their father's home to their husband's; they might work as servants for five to ten years before marrying. For women in the middle and upper classes, however, typically the only life choice other than to marry

was to enter the very restricted life of a religious convent.

The Renaissance girls who did marry had little say in who would be their marriage partner. Their parents could betroth them (engage them to be married) when they were young children, and the marriage ceremony could be held when they were only twelve. (The marriage age for boys was fourteen.) To create or affirm a political alliance, daughters of kings and other rulers could expect to be married to a complete stranger, possibly leaving home for a distant land where they did not speak the language. Wealthy landowning families also negotiated the marriages of their daughters without regard to their personal desires. Instead, these marriages were arranged by carefully weighing the value of the dowry (money or land) the woman would bring to the marriage as well as the ability of the husband's family to use this alliance to strengthen its political, economic, or social position.

According to the Renaissance ideal, the man was the head of the household. As Francesco Barbaro, of Venice, Italy, wrote in his treatise on marriage in 1416, "Let the husband give the orders and let the wife carry them out with a cheerful temper." [5] The Renaissance husband controlled—or was thought to control—every aspect of life within his household. His wife needed his permission for everything she did, even simply

During the Renaissance, noble families typically arranged the marriages of their children. This painting depicts the wedding of a young aristocratic couple.

to leave the house. Historians Sara Mendelson and Patricia Crawford explain:

> A wife could make no legal contract, except concerning her clothes and food. Her husband could sell her clothes. Her earnings were not her own, and she could neither sue nor be sued. Any inheritances of personal property she was due were her husband's, unless some specific protection had been made.[6]

Happy Marriages

Although young men and women had little choice in whom they would marry, writings from Renaissance times show that many husbands and wives loved each other. Englishwoman Lucy Hutchinson's memorial to her husband, written after his death, is a record of one happy Renaissance marriage. She admired her husband for the gentle, honorable way that he carried out his role as head of the household: "He governed by persuasion, which he never employed but to things honorable and profitable for herself [his wife, Lucy]; he loved her soul and honor more than her outside . . . all that she was was *him,* while he was here, and all that she is now is at best but his pale shade."[7]

Anne, Lady Fanshawe is another Renaissance woman whose marriage was happy and fulfilling. In her memorial to her husband, Anne emphasized the unity in spirit, outlook, and attitudes that she and her husband shared. Clearly this was a far deeper love than that which would simply lead to a relationship of mutual toleration and politeness:

Glory be to God we never had but one mind throughout our lives, our

This fifteenth-century Italian diptych shows an aristocratic couple. Certain Renaissance writings reflect genuine affection between husbands and wives.

souls were wrapped up in each other, our aims and designs one, our loves one, and our resentments one. We so studied one the other that we knew each other's mind by our looks; whatever was real happiness, God gave it me in him.[8]

Dangers to Wives

Yet the social and legal power given to Renaissance husbands over their wives could lead to cruelty and suffering. According to Mendelson and Crawford, "Society tolerated a great deal of violence against wives as a normal feature of domestic relations. The scriptural language about the patriarch's responsibility for 'lawful and reasonable correction' authorized men to beat their wives, children, and subordinates."[9]

Court records from 1566 have preserved the story of Englishwoman Judith Pollard, who "brought witnesses to court to tell of beatings 'in the dead time of night' which disturbed the neighborhood. Her husband had locked her out of the house on a cold January night; although she was pregnant and the neighbours had begged him to readmit her, he had refused."[10] On that winter night, Judith Pollard was taken in by a neighbor, Margaret Jones. Many Renaissance wives could have told a similar story.

Warning Women About the Dangers of Marriage

Lady Mary Chudleigh wrote a poem responding to the many works by male writers of the Renaissance, both for and against women and marriage. Lady Chudleigh's poem (quoted in Margaret J.M. Ezell, *The Patriarch's Wife*) represents a strong warning to women about the dangers to wives of the husband's dominant role in marriage, which Chudleigh calls "that fatal knot."

To the Ladies
Wife and Servant are the same,
But only differ in the Name:

For when that fatal knot is tied,
Which nothing, nothing can divide:
When she the word *obey* has said,
And Man by Law supreme is made,
Then all that's kind is laid aside,
And nothing left but State and
 Pride;

Then shun, oh! shun the wretched
 State,
And all the fawning flatterers hate:
Value your selves, and Men despise,
You must be proud, if you'll be wise.

Women of the Renaissance

Renaissance Women as Caregivers

For some women, the role of caregiver—seen in the Renaissance as acceptable because it was one element in the role of Good Wife—offered opportunities for service and work outside of their own household. Some caregivers served as domestic workers, while others nursed children, delivered babies, supervised charitable institutions, and provided many types of medical services.

Wet nurses provided a special type of child care. In this era, the only way to feed a newborn was with mother's milk, yet upper-class mothers almost never nursed their own children, instead hiring a wet nurse to care for them. Anne Mantell was in charge of the nursery of the Sidney family in England, and probably served as the wet nurse of the poet and diplomat Sir Philip Sidney. His biographer, Katherine Duncan-Jones, writes that in 1576, while preparing for a diplomatic mission to the Holy Roman Empire,

> Sidney found time to write to his father's steward, Robert Walker, to remind him that Mrs. Mantell's salary of £20 (quite a handsome rate for an upper servant) was due. His emphatic tone suggests that this was a matter that concerned him greatly: 'If you possibly may I pray you do this and you shall do me a great pleasure.' [11]

Wet nursing, open only to married women with good reputations, was relatively high-status work, especially compared with the job opportunities open to single women. As author Merry E. Wiesner points out:

> Many of these jobs were viewed as extensions of a woman's functions and tasks in the home—cleaning, cooking, laundering, caring for children and old people, nursing the sick, preparing bodies for burial, mourning the dead. They usually required no training beyond what a girl learned from her mother, and were poorly paid, with low status and no job security. [12]

Delivering Babies

A large group of caregivers worked as midwives, delivering babies. In this era, it was not considered appropriate for physicians, who were all men, to come into close contact with a woman patient's body. Wiesner explains the range of Renaissance midwives' duties:

> Cities and rulers took as great care with the regulation of midwives as they did with the regulation of physicians and surgeons. They did this because the midwife had an extremely important role, not only handling

This fifteenth-century painting shows a midwife and other attendants assisting a noblewoman after the birth of her child.

nearly every birth, but also performing additional medical services, distributing public welfare, serving various religious functions, and giving testimony in legal cases. [13]

One of the cities employing its own midwives and related caregivers was Nuremberg, Germany. As a Protestant city, Nurem-berg no longer had any Catholic convents, which had provided social services during the Middle Ages. Instead, the city itself provided health and welfare services to its residents, also hiring women to organize and oversee the delivery of these services. These were demanding positions with financial and managerial responsibilities corresponding to those of a modern hos-

Women of the Renaissance

pital administrator or social services manager. According to Wiesner, Nuremberg's *Ehrbare Frauen* (literally, "respected women") and, later, *Geschworene Weiber* (literally, "sworn-in wives"),

assigned midwives and distributed food and clothing to indigent [poor] mothers, as well as disciplining women they felt were not living up to their midwives' oath. They were responsible for making an annual report to the city council immediately after Easter, reporting any problems or deficiencies among the midwives. [14]

Women filled this semigovernmental role in hospitals and almshouses in many other European cities as well. Renaissance hospitals served much broader purposes than do today's medical centers. In the early modern era, hospitals were homes for people suffering from chronic illnesses, for poor women who were pregnant, for abandoned children, and for both children and adults who had a mental illness or a developmental disability. Wiesner describes the crucial role women had in running these institutions:

Women cooked, cleaned and cared for the patients, and also did administrative work and bookkeeping, led the patients in prayer, and carried out examinations for admissions. In the Netherlands, for example, widowed

Comforting Distressed Women

Elizabeth Walker was one of the upper-class women who saw charity as part of their role. Her husband's book, *The Holy Life of Mrs. Elizabeth Walker* (quoted in Sara Mendelson and Patricia Crawford, *Women in Early Modern England, 1550–1720*), tells about the charitable work she did to help poor people, especially women:

Another object of her painful charity . . . was women laboring with child, whom she would rise at any hour of the night to go out to, and carry with her what might be useful to them, having good skill and store of medicines always ready by her for such occasions; and there was scarcely ever any difficulty in that case round about, but recourse was made to her, both for advice and medicines; and, if might be with convenience, for her presence, which was always very acceptable and comfortable to the distressed women when the distance was such that she could afford [manage] it.

or married women often served as regentesses of almshouses, inspecting them daily, overseeing their operations, and contributing to the success of Dutch charity. In many cities throughout Europe women distributed poor relief to families in their own homes, with the city governments relying on the women's knowledge of their own neighborhoods to prevent fraud. [15]

In London, the governors of St. Bartholomew's Hospital recorded their gratitude to a woman hospital administrator, Matron Margaret Blague, "for her attendance and constant great pains about the poor . . . wherein she hath adventured herself to the great peril of her life." [16]

Louyse Bourgeois, Royal Midwife

One of the best-known Renaissance midwives was a Frenchwoman, Louyse Bourgeois, who lived from 1563 to 1636 and practiced in Paris. Her original training was as a lacemaker, but she learned about anatomy and surgery from her husband, Martin Boursier, and a well-known physician of the day, Ambroise Paré. Bourgeois became the royal midwife, delivering Marie de Médicis of the baby who would become King Louis XIII of France. Health care scholar Thomas G. Benedek says about this midwife, "One indication of her unusual independence was that she persistently used her maiden name, Bourgeois." [17]

Bourgeois, who supervised almost two thousand births, drew on her training and experience to write three books, one of which became a standard text and was translated into German and Dutch. She also wrote an attack on a group of male physicians who had issued a report on childbirth even though they had no medical training in this field. (At this time, formal medical training, which was for men only, was still based on the writings of ancient Greek scientists such as Galen, not on scientific research.)

These things are no better known to you than they were to your master Galen who, although he never had a wife and also attended few pregnant and child bearing women, yet took the liberty to dictate to a midwife how she should conduct herself in her duties. He also wrote a book about this subject in which, however, he betrays that he never knew anything about the uterus of a pregnant woman or about her afterbirth. [18]

Other Women Healers

Renaissance women also provided other types of healing services, even though they could learn only through personal expe-

Women tend to the needs of the sick in a hospital in Florence in this sixteenth-century painting.

rience or by observing the work of an experienced healer. In 1572, for example, the city of York permitted Isabel Warwike to be a healer because she had "skill in the science of surgery and has done good therein."[19] (In this era, unlike today, "surgery" meant relatively simple medical procedures such as treating skin diseases, pulling teeth, and lancing boils.)

Female healers often provided their services at no charge, seeing them as part of their expected womanly role or as charitable actions to help the poor and suffering. Nevertheless, male physicians, viewing women healers as competition, often criticized them harshly. Women healers could be accused of practicing witchcraft, especially since any medicines they administered might be considered "magic potions." Increasingly, Renaissance laws limited the ability of women to provide healing services. A 1529 regulation from Nuremberg reflects these negative attitudes:

The *Zuckermacherinnen* [women healers] and other old women, or whoever they are, make elixirs, tonics, and juices and give each one of them a special name, though they don't know what belongs in each of them, or how they are to be prepared; if

This page from a Renaissance book of medicines shows some of the spices and stones that were used to brew elixirs.

cil against a healer named Elizabeth Heyssin. Presumably some of the era's negative attitudes and assumptions concerning women in general, and specifically concerning women in competition with men, lay behind this complaint. Heyssin's defense of her work as a healer emphasizes her religious convictions—not her desire to make a profit—and her traditional womanly commitment to charitable caregiving:

> God in Heaven, who gave me soul and body, reason and understanding for which I have to thank him daily, gave me my skill at healing. I heal out of charity for the poor and needy ... [as is] done by honorable women not only here but also in other cities just as large and important as Memmingen. Such are fine things for women to do.[21]

they simply taste right to them, then they give it that name, sell the stuff, and deceive people with it. So from now on, no one is to sell these juices or elixirs unless they have let a doctor see the ingredients and recipe beforehand.[20]

In 1596, the male barbers and surgeons of another German city, Memmingen, brought a complaint before the city coun-

The procedures of Heyssin's trial took four months to complete. During this time, many residents of the city of Memmingen testified about Heyssin's charitable healing work and about her skill in curing the ailments from which they suffered. Grudgingly, therefore, the city council allowed Heyssin to continue her medical work, but with harsh restrictions designed to limit her

Women of the Renaissance

ability to compete with male healers and to assure that she observed Renaissance social expectations regarding a woman's behavior in public:

Elizabeth Heyssin is to be allowed to treat external wounds and sores in the same manner that she has been doing up til now, but only on women and children when they request it of her. She should absolutely not handle new wounds, bloodletting, or setting bones and should behave and handle herself with all possible modesty. Her daughter, though, is to be totally forbidden from practicing any kind of medicine. [22]

Renaissance women worked hard to care for their husbands, children, and neighbors. Some were unpaid domestic workers, and some earned wages or fees as caregivers. Furthermore, in their roles as daughters and wives, girls and women did many nondomestic types of work, especially tasks carried out in household workshops. These Renaissance businesses were regulated by trade groups called guilds.

Guild regulations often required the male "master" of a workshop to be married. He needed a wife to assume responsibility for feeding and clothing everyone in the household, including the servants and the workers in training, who lived with the family. The wife had business responsibilities as well, including helping with production, selling goods in the marketplace, and managing the workshop whenever her husband was away. Many Good Wives also carried out financial caregiving roles in a family business by purchasing raw materials for the workshop, by keeping its accounting records, and by collecting its debts. In the Renaissance era, however, these were seen as wifely tasks, not part of a career in business.

As a caregiver, the Renaissance Good Wife played an essential role in the welfare of her family—and often in its financial success as well. She bore and raised the children. She obtained and cooked the food that nourished everyone in the extended household. She worked to earn money or to help make a workshop profitable. In addition to all of these tasks, the Good Renaissance Wife helped to create a sense of warmth and love to unify and support her family.

Chapter 2:
Women at Work

Renaissance cultural expectations, which encouraged all women to take on the role of wife, restricted women's opportunities in business and the professions. In this era, however, many women were widowed or remained unmarried, and women headed one-quarter of all households. Not surprisingly, then, approximately three-quarters of all Renaissance women were employed. Further, records show that most women who did fill the role of Good Wife also worked to earn money, often alongside their husbands—even in such rough occupations as butcher, miner, and soldier. Generally women's work was low-skilled, low-status, and poorly paid; nevertheless, a few Renaissance women found ways to reach above the limited roles assigned to them and achieve success in business.

In medieval times, the ideal role for either a man or a woman—known as a vocation, or calling—was to live a spiritual life devoted to worshiping God. Men in this role were often priests or monks, while many of the women chose to be nuns. During the Renaissance, though, the rise of Protestant religions led to different views about vocations. Protestants placed a high value on the role of men in business but did not honor the paid work of women. In a significant change from medieval ideas, Protestants saw men's labor in the world, from farming to goldsmithing to weaving, as ways of honoring God and earning God's blessings.

The situation was very different for Renaissance women, who were seen as receiving the blessings of a vocation only in the roles of wife and mother. Although Renaissance women of almost all classes had countless responsibilities and worked very hard, carrying out these tasks did not earn them praise within their culture. Instead, the many types of women's work were taken as actions expected from any wife, in her role as helpmeet to her husband.

Women Workers in the Countryside

Among the hardest-working Renaissance women were agricultural laborers. About three-quarters of the population of Europe lived in the countryside, and most were poor. Rural men and women customarily performed different tasks, but women also did men's work, especially when the crops had to be harvested before bad weather could damage them. According to Wiesner:

A recent study of harvesting in seventeenth-century Yorkshire finds that women put in 38 percent of the time needed to bring in the grain. In areas where harvesting was done with a scythe [a sharp blade at the end of a long wooden handle, used to cut stalks of grain], women gathered and bound the grain and gleaned the fields [picked up grains that fell off the stalks], jobs that were actually physically more taxing than cutting because they involved constant stooping and bending. [23]

Records show rural women being paid for "weeding, sale of seeds, picking and

As this sixteenth-century painting of a money changer and his wife shows, Renaissance women often worked alongside their husbands in the family business.

setting [planting] strawberries, and relieving a servant who was sick." Other women did heavier tasks, including Widow Weller, who "was paid for cleaning a pond, ploughing a piece [of land] for oats, carrying fifteen loads of hay, and bringing in a load of loam [topsoil]."[24] While some farming tasks remained unchanged from medieval times, Renaissance women also cared for olive groves, harvested grapes, raised mulberry trees, fed the mulberry leaves to silkworms, and unwound the raw silk thread from the silkworms' cocoons. For agricultural work, women were paid about half what a man would earn. A meal was sometimes a significant part of the pay, and women laborers always received much less food than the men did.

The responsibilities of the countrywoman included tasks beyond housework and field labor. Historian Barbara Hanawalt writes: "In addition to the tasks of running the household the wife produced and trained the new work force, gathered nuts and berries, sent sons out to fish and daughters to get water, cared for the garden and domesticated animals, and engaged in a number of supplemental economic

Men and women worked side by side to harvest grain. Usually men cut the grain while women gathered it into sheaves.

Regulating the Market Women

Merry E. Wiesner, a historian and author of *Working Women in Renaissance Germany,* has sought out information on working women by tracing references in the regulations and ordinances of German cities. These laws give some sense of what life was like for market women selling goods from an open-air stall:

> During the last part of the fifteenth century, a number of cities expanded their ordinances. That from 1485 in Frankfurt forbade women who sold used clothing to sell harnesses or leather goods and required that "every third penny" they made be turned over to the city, an extremely high level of taxation.... They were forbidden to sell before eleven in the morning, or seven on market days, and specifically told not to "bring harm to anyone's honor," in other words, to call anyone names or accuse a person of anything.

> Cities relaxed their restrictions on selling once or twice during the year, during special fairs or festivals, and the women sold metalwork, spices, weapons, furs, new clothing, and glass along with their usual wares. They often kept selling these extras once the fair was over, until the group who normally sold them—tinsmiths, spice dealers, armamentmakers [men who made armor, swords, and other weapons], furriers, tailors, or whoever—complained.

activities." [25] Women supplemented the family income by making and selling butter, cheese, vinegar, yeast, smoked meats, and soap. When they traveled to a market, women bought small items like candles, pins, and ribbons to resell upon returning to their villages. Englishwoman Katherine Windham's account book reveals that she "'bought of Mrs Pooly' soap, apples, eggs, butter, and a shoe brush." [26]

Also laboring in the countryside were Renaissance women miners. They appear in artwork of the time, writes Wiesner, that shows "women carrying ore, wood, and salt, sorting and washing ore, and preparing charcoal briquets for use in smelting [melting ore to extract metal]." [27] Mining was one of the jobs that required the labor of both husband and wife, though the husband received the pay—and the recognition. In the case of mining, the man would be paid for each basket of ore he produced, but his wife and children had to break it apart and wash it after he carried it up from underground. Washing, in this case a much heavier form of labor even than laundry, was still "woman's work."

Slaves, Beggars, and Street Vendors

Slavery and serfdom had disappeared from the western European countryside by the early modern era, but some wealthy city families still owned a household slave, almost always a woman. Italian masters purchased Slavs—girls and women from the Slavic peoples of eastern Europe—who had been captured from their homes, while Portuguese and Spanish masters owned slaves from northern and western Africa. Renaissance slaves were often given tasks requiring considerable responsibility and the ability to work independently. One Italian slave, "black-haired Caterina," had been captured as a nine-year-old from Circassia (in southeast Russia) and sold to Francesco Giovanni of Florence. Records from a lawsuit reveal that when Caterina was eighteen, her master went on a journey and "entrusted the house and children to her in his absence."[28]

Many other Renaissance women lived in such poverty that they could survive only by begging. Typically, widows and abandoned wives were unable to earn enough money to support themselves and their children. Spinning wool into thread—women's traditional occupation—was very low-paid work. One German beggar petitioned the city of Frankfurt for welfare,

saying, "What little I make at spinning will not provide enough for my own bread."[29] Cities made continuing efforts to address the problems of women beggars, but often the regulations served only as punishments.

Ellen Daniel was forced to become a beggar in 1614 when Turkish pirates raided the city of Baltimore, Ireland. The pirates seized her husband, Richard, and sold him into slavery. Ellen was granted a license by the city "to beg for two years to support herself and five children, and accumulate sufficient funds to redeem [him]."[30] Yet beggar women were often treated even more harshly. According to government records from 1659, the city of Dublin, Ireland, set up "a large cage . . . in the corn market to imprison all beggars, idle women and maids selling apples and oranges."[31]

It was only a slight step up from begging, but selling apples and oranges on the streets, or peddling small items like writing materials, was another way for uneducated women to scrape together a living. Anne Keene was a witness in a court case and thus left a record of her work. The twenty-six-year-old wife of a ship's armorer, Keene testified that she "uses the market and quays [docks] and sells garden ware."[32] In this way she earned about one shilling a day. Mendelson and Crawford found that

women in the towns had a similar economy of makeshifts to those in the countryside, combining house-keeping and child-care with whatever paid employment they could find. Typically, they were servants in youth, earning their best wages as needleworkers in middle age, and charring [cleaning], washing, nursing, and hawking [selling items on the street] in old age. [33]

Involuntary Service

Even if a Renaissance woman could find a way to support herself, she risked arrest if she were not under the authority of a man, either a father, a husband, or a master. Most European countries or cities had laws requiring an unmarried woman to find a position as a servant, in which she would come under the control of a master. Poor women without a position "in service" also lost their children, whom the authorities took when they reached the age of seven and placed in households to work as servants. Mendelson and Crawford discuss the English law:

> Poor single women might have little choice of employment. By the 1563 Statute of Artificers [Workers], all unmarried women between 12 and 40 could be ordered into service. Subsequently, all over England, civic authorities worked at putting the statute into effect. In Norwich in the

A Good Wife (center) sells grapes, pears, and other fruit to a servant girl (right).

1630s, Cecily Robinson was sent to Bridewell [a women's prison] until she was put into service or her father fetched her. In 1654, Mary Plumstead was ordered to find herself a master within the month or be confined to the House of Correction until she was hired. [34]

Closing the Doors Against Women in Trade

European economies worsened during the sixteenth century. In response, governmental authorities often enacted harsh measures like England's Statute of Artificers against poor women. Yet, due to the effects of the era's wars and financial depres-

Busied in the Merchandise Trade

Glückel of Hameln, whose name means "little piece of luck," was a Jewish woman born in Hamburg, Germany, in 1646. When she was two years old, all of the Jews were expelled from Hamburg, and Glückel's family moved to Hamelin ("Hameln" in German). This was only one of many persecutions that Jews experienced in Renaissance times. Jews were sometimes forced to leave an entire country and become wanderers through other parts of Europe. Forbidden to own land or enter a trade, Jews had to make their living as traders and bankers. For all these reasons, Jewish women experienced different dangers—and had different business opportunities—than typical women of the time.

Glückel was married at fourteen to a man named Chaim, who traded in jewelry and precious metals. They had thirteen children, of whom twelve lived to adulthood. In her memoirs Glückel discusses her close and happy marriage, and her involvement in Chaim's enterprises: "My husband took advice from nobody else, and did nothing without our talking it over together" (quoted in Theodore K. Rabb, *Renaissance Lives*). After her husband died, Glückel carried on the business:

I busied myself in the merchandise trade, selling every month to the amount of five or six hundred Reichsthalers. I went twice a year to the Brunswick fair, and each time made several thousands in profit. . . . My business prospered. I bought goods from Holland; I bought nicely in Hamburg, and disposed of the goods in a store of my own. I never spared myself: summer and winter I was out on my travels, and I rushed about the city. I maintained a lively trade in seed pearls, selected them and sorted them, and resold in towns where there was a good demand.

sion, women continued to fall into poverty. Changing trade patterns and the movement of production from household workshops to factories also caused women increasing difficulty in finding employment.

In the hard economic times of the sixteenth century, costs rose and earnings fell. As a result, guilds sought ways to limit competition and preserve the incomes of their members. Frequently, working women were the targets of these restrictive measures. The male-controlled guilds prohibited women from making and selling goods; in addition, they forbade masters to train any women, even their own wives and daughters, as workers. Historian Judith M. Bennett writes, "In 1584 . . . a jury in Manchester [England] noted that unmarried women baked, brewed, and pursued other trades 'to the great hurt of the poor inhabitants having wives and children.'" [35] The jury did not address the fact that unmarried women, who might also be supporting children, needed incomes as well.

Losing a Traditional Means of Earning a Living

Renaissance social and economic trends gradually closed even traditional women's trades. One example is ale brewing, a trade that had been open to unmarried women and also to wives who brewed to supplement the family income. Ale was the staple beverage in medieval northern Europe; it was relatively easy to make but did not keep well. Thus many medieval women brewed it frequently, in small batches, and sold it to their neighbors.

In the Renaissance era, the introduction of beer, which is fermented like ale but stays fresh longer and is brewed in large quantities, had the effect of taking this small work opportunity away from women. Owning a large beer brewery required capital, and women were unable to borrow money. In addition, the large batches of beer had to be sold to customers beyond the immediate neighborhood—a difficult practice for women, who were expected to remain at home. Furthermore, managing a brewery required leadership of a largely male workforce, as the tasks involved in brewing beer had become "men's work." Bennett explains:

One estimate from 1636 suggests that a beerbrewer employed almost two dozen workers, including three clerks, a master brewer and an underbrewer, four tun men [who attended the brewing vats], a stoker [who fueled the brewery's furnace], a miller, two coopers [who built beer barrels], six draymen [wagon drivers], two stable workers, and a hog man [who used a heavy tool called a hog to stir the malt]. [36]

Some medieval women were able to continue a business such as a brewery after

A group of men drink in a tavern in this fourteenth-century English illustration.

A 1576 London court case tells the story of one widow, Margery Draper, who struggled to maintain a brewery on her own. An employee, Thomas Hobson, who was the clerk responsible for the accounts of the business, sued his new mistress. Draper responded that Hobson was cheating her and that he had "most shamefully, wickedly and horribly"[37] tried to force one of her daughters to marry him. Hobson probably saw marrying a Draper daughter as a step toward taking over the business. Clearly Margery Draper was unable to exert adequate authority over Hobson, and probably over some of the other men working in her brewery as well.

Wiltenburg sums up the economic changes affecting women in Renaissance times:

> During the sixteenth and seventeenth centuries, women suffered a substantial decline in economic power across wide areas of Europe, as population pressure and economic distress led to increasing restrictions on women's work, and as advancing market organization tended to remove control of production from the household. In trades controlled by guilds, early modern regulations frequently reserved skilled work for male workers. In areas outside guild control, where production was moving away from household organization to rely increasingly on

their husbands' death. Yet social and economic changes occurring in the early modern era also closed off this opportunity for women. Renaissance culture made it very difficult for a woman, even if she inherited a business from her husband, to maintain the needed position of authority over the male workers.

Women of the Renaissance

wage labor, women tended to lose managerial responsibilities that had fallen to them in household workshops. [38]

Success Stories

Against this backdrop of increasing cultural limitations and financial struggle, a few successful businesswomen stand out boldly. Elizabeth Beaulacre of Geneva, Switzerland, was one of the most successful entrepreneurs of her generation. Widowed in 1641 when she was only twenty-eight, Beaulacre assumed management of her husband's small dry-goods firm, transforming it into one of the largest businesses in Geneva. Beaulacre employed hundreds of workers, who spun gold thread and created decorations from this precious material. At her death she left the second-largest personal fortune on record in that city during Renaissance times.

Another successful widow was Frenchwoman Benoîte Penet. A butcher's daughter, she worked with her husband, who was also a butcher, while raising her four daughters. After her husband died in 1540, Benoîte continued buying cattle at the market in Lyon, supervising the employees who slaughtered them, and selling the meat to Bear Inn, which was kept by another husband-and-wife team, Michael Hiberlin and Katherine Fichet.

Equally successful were eight different women in Lyon who ran large publishing enterprises. Lyon was one of the largest cities in Renaissance France and was a center of commerce and industry; Renaissance writer Joachim Du Bellay noted that there were "so many bankers, printers, armorers, thicker than the flowers in the fields." [39]

Through their labor, Renaissance women made significant contributions to the economies of Europe.

Yet in 1548 when King Henri II visited the city, no women were allowed to take part in the ceremony that welcomed him, which included a parade of craftsmen wearing the costumes of their guilds. Lyon publisher Jeanne Giunta referred to the attitudes limiting women's participation in business when she wrote:

Being of the female sex did not turn me from the enterprise of publishing, nor the fact that it be more a manly office. . . . It is not new or unheard of for women to have such a trade, and one can find many of us who exercise not only the typographical art, but others more difficult and arduous, and who obtain thereby the highest of praise. [40]

Lyon publisher Louise Giraud, wife of humanist scholar Etienne Dolet, had a

Women in the Military

Women and children were a significant part of Renaissance armies, often in numbers close to the number of men soldiers. In his article "Women and Military Institutions in Early Modern Europe: A Reconnaissance," historian Barton C. Hacker writes that "women in armies were not only normal, they were vital. Armies could not have functioned as well, perhaps could not have functioned at all, without the service of women." Often condemned as camp followers—little better than prostitutes—women in Renaissance armies did much the same work as other women of the time. Whether they were in the garrison or marching on a campaign, women cooked, cleaned, washed, and nursed, along with bearing and raising their children.

Hacker quotes a passage from a military book written in 1598 by Leonhard Fronsperger that reveals the demands commonly made on military women, as well as the harsh way they were seen. Advising the military commander, Fronsperger wrote:

He must see that the whores and loose fellows keep clean the latrines, and further that they wait upon their masters faithfully and that they are kept occupied when necessary with cooking, sweeping, washing and especially attendance on the sick; and that they never refuse either on the field or in the garrison, running, pouring out, fetching food and drink, knowing how to behave mostly with regard to the needs of others and taking it in turns to do what is necessary according to orders.

well-known printing shop, the Sign of the Hatchet. Under Giraud's leadership the business published thirteen editions from 1542 to 1544, while Dolet was in prison for heresy (expressing illegal religious beliefs). The religious controversies of the sixteenth century also marked the life of another woman printer in Lyon, Mie Roybet. She and her husband, Bartholémy Frein, kept a tavern in addition to a printing press. Widowed in 1556, Roybet continued both businesses. She was imprisoned for printing material advocating religious tolerance, "certain books in the French language touching matters of the Christian religion, without privilege and permission of the Faculty of Theology of Paris."[41] Upon her release a few months later, Roybet continued working in her printing business and running her tavern as well.

The Pattern of Women's Work—and the Exceptions

The women of Renaissance Europe worked hard, and their labor was essential to the economies of their regions. Under great difficulties women contributed to the incomes of their households—or supported themselves and their children unaided. Yet the picture of increasing restrictions on women's opportunities must be painted broadly enough to take in the exceptions discovered by today's historians, who have taken a new look at the historical documents. As Wiesner says:

> Of course . . . there were women who worked in nearly every craft in some city at some time, but almost all of these were widows, wives, daughters, or maids. The few who were not were clearly exceptions, although it is interesting to discover that there were women who ran foundries, shod horses, shipped sheet metal, and made armor. In every city there were always a few women operating independently making needles, rings, measures, thimbles, and other small articles out of iron and tin.[42]

The labor of Renaissance women helped build the economies and establish the business practices of today's societies. Very few of these women received recognition in their own lifetimes for their work or business skills. Yet recent research into Renaissance documents has shown that women living in towns and cities throughout Europe played significant roles in shaping the commercial culture of the modern world.

Chapter 3: Women in Religious Life

For centuries during the Middle Ages the church had barred women from most leadership positions, and in Renaissance times no women (except heads of convents) were involved in its financial or political affairs. Yet within the Renaissance climate of intense religious dissent and dramatic change, a few women found ways to make their voices heard and to play leadership roles. While some Renaissance women found their lives limited by the Protestant emphasis on the authority of the male head of the household, others took on the role of social or religious reformer, creating new forms of community. As Wiesner writes, "The Protestant Reformation both expanded and diminished women's opportunities."[43]

Cultural changes also affected women's religious lives. One of these was the scholarly and religious effort in the sixteenth century that led to the translation of the Bible into the different European languages, and its publication in relatively inexpensive editions through the new technology of the printing press. In medieval times, the Bible had been available to European peoples only in Latin, and each precious volume had to be copied by hand. Few women could read Latin in the Middle Ages, and even fewer had access to a Bible. During the Renaissance, however, a significant minor-

This fifteenth-century painting depicts a group of woman at prayer.

ity of women gained literacy in their own languages. They began to read the Bible and to find in this highly respected source many passages supporting their efforts to participate in religious and charitable life.

Powerful rulers and city governments controlled many of the social, legal, and religious changes occurring during the Reformation, but sometimes mobs of ordinary people, including women, took action to defend their beliefs. As Wiesner writes:

During this period, many groups and individuals tried to shape the new religious institutions. Sometimes this popular pressure took the form of religious riots, in which women and men destroyed paintings, statues, stained-glass windows or other objects that symbolized the old religion, or protected such objects from destruction at the hands of government officials; in 1536 at Exeter in England, for example, a group of women armed with shovels and pikes attacked workers who had been hired by the government to dismantle a monastery.[44]

Nuns in an Era of Religious Change

An institution remaining from the Middle Ages was the convent, a place where many women continued in Renaissance times to live out their lives as nuns. Catholic fami-

The Virgin Mary appears as a Renaissance nun in this fifteenth-century painting.

lies that could not or would not provide a dowry could force a daughter to become a nun. Frequently this occurred amid "tears and wailing,"[45] according to an Italian government document. Yet a high percentage of upper-class daughters became nuns, and some less wealthy girls lived in convents as servants, called *conversae*. In Italy in 1552, 13 percent of all women did not fill the role of Good Wife but were nuns or *conversae*.

One hundred years later, records from one Italian city, Venice, count three thousand nuns, "some 3 percent of the whole population." [46]

Women who chose to enter a convent and devote their lives to spirituality had been honored in medieval times. With the rise of Protestantism, the number and importance of convents diminished, yet in areas that remained Catholic these women's religious institutions continued. The strong appeal of the cloistered life for some women is reflected in the words of Camilla da Varano, who entered the convent of St. Clare in Urbino, Italy, in 1481: "I found the sweetest singing of pious prayers, the beauty of good examples, secret chambers of divine grace and heavenly gifts." [47] While nuns like Camilla found satisfaction in convent life, others reached beyond the walls of their convent to become religious leaders and reformers. Some remained Catholic, but others found different spiritual pathways.

Teresa of Avila (Spain), one of the most famous women of the Renaissance era, never advocated that women step out of their accustomed roles within the Catholic Church. Yet she was a powerful leader and reformer. Even as a child she had a dynamic personality and a strong religious faith. Born in 1515 into a family of twelve children, she was closest to her brother Roderigo. In her spiritual autobiography she wrote,

It was Roderigo whom I most loved. We used to read the lives of saints together, and when I read of the martyrdoms suffered by saintly women for God's sake, I thought they had purchased grace very cheaply. I had a keen desire to die as they had done, in order to attain as quickly as possible the great blessings which, as I read, were laid up in Heaven. I used to discuss with my brother how we could become martyrs. We agreed to go off to the country of the Moors, begging our bread, so that they might behead us there. [48]

At one point Teresa and Roderigo actually set off from home to begin this quest. As they walked down what they thought was the road to the country of the Moors, however, they met one of their uncles, and he took them back home to their parents.

Later, as a nun in the Carmelite convent at Avila, Teresa spent many years experiencing religious visions, developing a sense of closeness with the divine, and coming to believe that she had a direct relationship with God. Teresa became convinced that it was important for the Carmelite convents of Spain to return to their early purity, so she and a few helpers began traveling throughout the country to spread this message. Once, when her carriage got stuck in the mud, Teresa was said to have looked toward heaven and

"More Faith than Men"

Teresa of Avila wrote *The Way of Perfection* in the 1560s. In this passage, translated by Alison Weber in *Teresa of Avila and the Rhetoric of Femininity,* Teresa questions the limitations imposed on women by the insistence of Renaissance culture on their chastity, obedience, and silence.

Lord of my soul, you did not hate women when You walked in the world; rather you favored them always with much pity and found in them as much love and more faith than men. Is it not enough, Lord, that the world has intimidated us . . . so that we may not do anything worthwhile for you in public?

The Catholic Church canonized Teresa shortly after her death, but removed these words before publishing her book.

Saint Teresa of Avila questioned the limits Renaissance society placed on women.

exclaimed, "God, if this is the way you treat your friends, no wonder you have so few of them!"[49]

The male authorities of the Catholic Church were unsure how to deal with the actions of this dynamic nun, preferring that women approach God through formal rituals and prayers led by a (male) priest. They were disturbed by Teresa's claim to have a direct relationship with God. The pope sent a papal nuncio (ambassador) to Spain to investigate Teresa's activities. In his report, the papal nuncio referred to her as a "restless gadabout, a disobedient and obstinate woman, who invented wicked doctrines and called them devotion . . . and taught others against the commands of St. Paul, who had forbidden women to teach."[50] Yet the Catholic authorities eventually accepted Teresa's spiritual leadership and honored her with sainthood shortly after her death in 1582.

Maintaining a Spiritual Pattern of Life

Nuns whose convents lay in Protestant lands were forced to make difficult decisions about how to live. Most nuns were from upper-class families and were accustomed to a higher status than they would be able to enjoy in the only equivalent role open to them in a Protestant area: wife of a clergyman. Protestant churches did not have convents, and Protestant communities offered no roles for women that could provide the privacy, dignity, and respect

The Virgin Mary and the Holy Women lament the death of Christ in this fifteenth-century painting.

often earned by Catholic nuns for their spiritual lives.

The nuns living in the convent at Vadstena, Sweden, for example, were members of the royal family and did not wish to change their cloistered way of life when their country adopted Protestantism in the 1540s. Wiesner writes that the Swedish monarch

> attempted to convince the nuns to accept Protestantism willingly, but the nuns resisted, stuffing wool and wax in their ears when they were forced to attend Lutheran services. The convent survived until the 1590s, when royal patience gave out; the nuns were then forcibly evicted and the convent's treasures and library confiscated.[51]

As abbess of Quendlinburg (in today's Germany), Anna von Stolberg took a more pragmatic approach. In 1540, when the land surrounding the area she ruled became Lutheran, Anna converted, but she retained many of the structures that had been established by the Catholic Church—which continued to extend privileges and send support. As abbess of this large institution, Anna governed an area that also included nine Catholic churches and two monasteries. She forced all of the priests to convert and turned one of the monasteries into a school for both boys and girls.

This fifteenth-century illuminated manuscript depicts a group of women building the wall that will isolate their spiritual community from the world.

A number of other convents made similar changes, surviving into the nineteenth century as organizations for unmarried women. As Wiesner points out:

> The distinction between Protestant and Catholic that is so important in understanding the religious and intellectual history of sixteenth-century Europe may have ultimately been less important to the women who lived in convents or other communal groups than the distinction between their pattern of life and that of the majority of lay women. . . . The Protestant championing of marriage and family life, which some nuns accepted with great enthusiasm as a message of liberation

from the convent, was viewed by others as a negation of the value of the life they had been living; thus they did all in their power to continue in their chosen path.[52]

Women's Communities

Seeking ways of keeping apart from the challenges of the world and the demands of marriage, women in the Netherlands created another pattern for living as a spiritual group. Founded by a religious reform movement known as the Devotio Moderna, this alternative way of life enabled unmarried and widowed women to gather into houses run by the Sisters of the Common Life. Unlike nuns in a convent, the Sisters of the Common Life did not take religious vows. They earned their living by the traditional women's occupations of copying manuscripts, teaching children, and weaving. One of their houses had six hundred residents.

In Brescia, Italy, Angela Merici founded a community similar to the Sisters of the Common Life called the Company of St. Ursula. This community survived from its founding in 1535 to 1810. Earning their own living by teaching or weaving, the unmarried women in the Company of St. Ursula received approval from the pope in spite of their independent way of living. They provided care to those most in need in Renaissance society: the poor, the sick, casualties of war, and orphans. Women in Spain and France also founded non-monastic societies dedicated to helping the poor.

Wives of Clergy: Filling a New Role

Women who filled the new role of Good Wife of a Protestant clergyman were in an unprecedented position. These women had no models to follow and sometimes faced hostility from people who could not accept their marriages as legitimate. (Priests of the Catholic Church had not been permitted to marry since the early Middle Ages.) In addition, Protestant clergymen, especially those who had previously been priests, sometimes failed to embrace their addi-

tional roles as head of a household and father of a family. As unmarried priests, they had had no family responsibilities and were accustomed to having their food and housing supplied by others. Yet Renaissance society looked to these clergy families to exemplify the perfect family unit, and, as historians Mendelson and Crawford note, clergy wives were seen as "exemplifying the godly ideal of good womanhood."[53] Many women in the position struggled to provide for their families and meet society's high expectations.

One minister's wife, Elizabeth Walker, took a serious approach to fulfilling the godly ideal for a Renaissance woman. Mendelson and Crawford write that to maintain her own spiritual life while also carrying out household tasks expected of a housewife, Walker "slept fewer hours so she could be up at 4 a.m. to spend time at her private prayers before her busy daily round of supervising children and servants and assisting neighbors."[54]

Godly as they were, these clergy wives typically agreed with the view of society that their demanding domestic work was "worldly" and therefore not worthy of respect. They struggled to find time for personal prayer and for charitable work. As Protestant clergy wife Sarah Savage wrote, "Through the necessity of my outward affairs, my secret [personal spiritual] duties are commonly limited. I have been ready to fear that I have declined in grace."[55]

Writing in Defense of Their Faith

In the face of the Renaissance command that women be silent, women in the Reformation era strove to gain the right to express their religious convictions. The admonition to keep silent had a basis in several passages of the Bible, including words ascribed to Paul in the Book of Timothy, ordering women not to teach or preach. Women authors of the Reformation felt it necessary to address—and overcome—the limitations placed on them by this prohibition.

"A Course Never Thought of Before"

In 1616, devout Catholic Mary Ward received provisional approval from Pope Paul V to establish the Institute of the Blessed Virgin Mary in the Netherlands. Ward hoped that the women in this institute could act as missionaries and help reestablish Catholicism in her native country, England. She said, "It seems that the female sex also in its own measure, should and can . . . undertake something more than ordinary in this great common spiritual undertaking" (quoted in Merry E. Wiesner, *Women and Gender in Early Modern Europe*).

Ward's missionary plans proved to be too bold for the church hierarchy to accept, though, and instead she set up houses throughout Europe where women lived and ran schools for boys and girls. Asking for permission to travel and raise funds for these schools without supervision by a man, Ward acknowledged that this was "a course never thought of before."

Yet she argued that "there is no such difference between men and women that women may not do great things as we have seen by the examples of many saints." Ward accepted men's leadership of the family and the Church. Yet (as quoted in Margaret L. King, *Women of the Renaissance*), Ward asked,

In all other things, wherein are we so inferior to other creatures that they should term us "but women"? For what think you of this word, "but women," as if we were in all things inferior to some other creature which I suppose to be a man! Which I dare be bold to say is a lie.

The leaders of the Catholic Church did not accept Ward's ideas and arguments. They put her in prison and closed down the homes for women that she had set up.

Argula von Grumbach, a German woman who wrote eight books in 1523 and 1524, argued: "I am not unfamiliar with Paul's words that women should be silent in church but when I see that no man will or can speak, I am driven by the word of God when he said, 'He who confesses me on earth, him will I confess, and he who denies me, him will I deny.'"[56] Ursula Weyda, also a German, wrote a pamphlet in 1524 in which she, like Argula, drew on different Bible passages to support her right to express her religious views: "If all women were forbidden to speak, how could daughters prophesy as Joel [a biblical prophet] predicted? Although St. Paul forbade women to preach in churches and instructed them to obey their husbands, what if the churches were full of liars?"[57]

Marie Dentière was a Reformation religious leader who had previously had a position of leadership as the abbess of a Catholic convent in Geneva. In a letter to Marguerite d'Angoulême, queen of Navarre, Dentière defended the active participation of women in the new religious institutions:

> I ask, didn't Jesus die just as much for the poor illiterates and the idiots as for the shaven, tonsured [with their hair shaven from the tops of their heads], and mighty lords [that is, monks and priests]? Did he only say, "Go, preach my Gospel to the wise lords and grand doctors"? Did he not say, "To all"? Do we have two Gospels, one for men and the other for women? . . . For we ought not, any more than men, hide and bury within the earth that which God has . . . revealed to us women.[58]

Dentière received strong support for this position from Katherine Zell of Strasbourg, Germany, who worked actively for the Reformation. Zell asked that Dentière's ideas be judged "not according to the standards of a woman, but according to the standards of one whom God has filled with the Holy Spirit."[59] After the devastation of the Peasant's War, Zell exercised her leadership skills in charitable work, managing "the care and feeding of three thousand refugees, including the wives and children of the slaughtered."[60] Late in her life, Zell wrote an open letter to the citizens of her city, offering her perspective on her life of service as a clergy wife:

> The work which I carried on both in the house and out is known both by those who already rest in God and those who are still living, how I helped to establish the Gospel, took in the exiled, comforted the homeless refugees, furthered the church, preaching and the schools. God will remember even if the world may forget or did not notice.[61]

In general, Renaissance people did not grant Zell's wish for women like Dentière and eventually silenced those who spoke out. Argula's husband was ordered to see that she stopped publishing her writings, and other women writers of the Reformation had similar experiences.

Founders of Charities

Charitable work was a traditional part of the role of religious women. The religious changes of the Renaissance era opened opportunities for new kinds of charitable work to some women, while closing off some avenues for service, such as joining a convent (if they lived in a Protestant land). Some of the Renaissance women whose charitable work is known to history today were accustomed to exercising power, like Diane de Poitiers, while others, like Elizabeth Kraus, rose from poor beginnings and endowed charities to assist others like themselves.

Diane de Poitiers spent twenty-three years as mistress of, and adviser to, King Henri II of France. After his death she retired to Anet, in the French countryside, where she applied her energy and leadership skills to a wide range of charitable projects, many of which were for the benefit of girls and women. Diane founded four social service institutions: "a hospital, a nursery for abandoned infants, a home for young women in trouble, and another for homeless women."[62] Addressing the

Diane de Poitiers founded several charitable institutions for women in the sixteenth century.

needs of the women living nearby, she established training courses for midwives, who previously had worked principally in cities. Seeing the difficulties that rural girls experienced in finding a husband, Diane set up a fund to grant them dowries.

Elizabeth Kraus, another woman of energy and leadership ability, was born into a peasant family but came to the city of Nuremberg as a ten-year-old orphan. Working as a maid, she earned a dowry and was able to marry a merchant named Konrad Kraus. Together they built up a fortune, based on his business, their real estate investments, and her work as *Findelmutter*

A Missionary to Poor Women

Luisa de Carvajal defied the restrictions that the Church and society in general placed on women's activities and became a Catholic missionary to England. In *Women and Gender in Early Modern Europe,* Merry E. Wiesner recounts how this devout Spanish woman traveled to London and lived in the residence of the Spanish ambassador. At first Luisa was successful in her mission, reaching poor women by acting as a mid-wife for them and helping to care for their children. She also set up a disguised convent. Eventually Luisa's activities, carried out under the apparent protection of the Spanish ambassador, were discovered by the (Protestant) archbishop of Canterbury. The Spanish government was embarrassed by this revelation and demanded that she return to Spain. However, Luisa died before she could be forced to leave England.

("foundling mother"), or head of Nuremberg's orphanage. Wiesner writes that the widowed Elizabeth died in 1639, leaving

> six houses and monetary capital of 79,000 florins [German currency], with the whole estate estimated at over 127,000 florins. Her will set this up as an endowment for the children of the orphanage, to provide them with a yearly feast and day-to-day necessities. The fund was the largest Protestant endowment in all of Germany. [63]

Women of the Renaissance endowed or led a variety of charitable organizations, including Nuremberg's Arme Kindbetterin Almosen (Donations for Poor Expectant Mothers) and Guldener Truncks (Golden Chest). Established in 1427 by Ottilia Kress and her husband Hilpot, Guldener Truncks was an endowment, a fund whose investment income was used to help orphan girls and servants by providing them with a dowry and wedding garments. Other cities in Germany had similar funds, but only Nuremberg's continued to be administered by a woman throughout the early modern era.

Protestant or Catholic, Renaissance women were swept up in the era's religious changes. The spirit of reform led Catholic women to make extraordinary efforts to improve the spirituality and religious practices of their convents. The blossoming of new ideas led Protestant women to read, learn, and strive for leadership in the evolving religious institutions being set up throughout Europe. In all this change, women's commitment to charity and desire to live honorable, useful lives remained a constant.

Chapter 4:
Renaissance Queens

As in the medieval era, during the Renaissance many European countries, including France, Spain, England, and Scotland, were kingdoms. Their kings were absolute rulers believed to have been appointed by God, and both tradition and law dictated the royal succession. Men had precedence over women, and the king's eldest son was his natural heir. A woman could inherit a kingdom only if the king had no male heir, and even then there was no guarantee that, once crowned, she could exert real authority. The Renaissance culture of male power and female subservience still applied at the highest levels of society, and even a queen was expected to defer to her male relatives and counselors. In addition, because wives had to obey their husbands, a queen who married risked giving up her authority to her husband. Nonetheless, while some Renaissance queens were simply figureheads or the political pawns of men, others took power into their own hands and played a central role in Renaissance events.

Pawns in the Succession Game

When a king died, it was not always clear who would inherit the throne. Women who had a claim to the throne were often used by the men around them as a means to seize power. The English noblewoman Lady Jane Grey found herself in this position when she was still a teenager—and lost her life as a result.

Jane's cousin Edward VI was the only son of King Henry VIII of England. Although Edward was not yet ten years old when his father died, as a male he preceded his older half sisters Mary and Elizabeth Tudor in the line of succession. The boy king was controlled, however, by his adviser, the ambitious duke of Northumberland. When Edward became seriously ill, Northumberland persuaded him to name Lady Jane Grey as his successor. Jane was Northumberland's daughter-in-law, and she was a Protestant. By having her named as future queen, Northumberland hoped both to retain his own powerful position and to prevent the Catholic sister, Mary, from ruling England.

Jane was fifteen when Edward died. When she was suddenly told that she was to be queen, she tried to refuse, saying, "The crown is not my right and pleaseth me not. The Lady Mary is the rightful heir."[64] But her objections were swept aside by Northumberland, and her parents commanded her to obey him. Mary Tudor, however, commanded widespread support, and it was soon clear that she, not Jane, would be the next queen. Just nine days after being proclaimed queen, Jane told her father she was withdrawing her claim, saying, "Out of obedience to you and my mother, I have grievously sinned. Now I willingly relinquish the crown."[65] Although she had not wished to be a part of this power grab, she paid with her life: Along with her husband and father-in-law, she was sentenced to death for high treason, and beheaded.

Renaissance Europe

Depicted as Equals

To reinforce their position, Renaissance kings and queens were careful to convey an image of power. They dressed to stand out from the rest of the court, always appeared to the public in majestic surroundings, and took care that every depiction—whether in a portrait or on a coin—showed them at their best.

Isabella of Castile had a further concern: She wanted to ensure that her equal status with her husband, Ferdinand of Aragon, was reflected in depictions of the couple. In *Cultural Atlas of the Renaissance,* C.F. Black explains how one portrait of Ferdinand and Isabella fulfilled Isabella's hopes: "They are shown face-to-face to stress the strict equality of their powers—traditionally a queen would be portrayed behind her spouse

Queen Isabella of Spain demanded that all coinage reflect her equal status with the king.

and facing the same way. Isabella expressly stipulated in her marriage contract that this was to be the design used on coinage."

Negotiating Her Share of Power

Although a wife—even when she was a queen—was expected to obey her husband, some Renaissance queens refused to give up power to their husbands. Isabella I, queen of Castile (one of several kingdoms in Renaissance Spain), took a series of strong actions to keep, and exert, the power she would inherit.

Isabella, who was born in 1451, was not a likely heir to her father's kingdom because he had two sons. Her much older half brother, Henry, did become king, but he was an ineffective ruler, and powerful Castilian noblemen rebelled against him, supporting instead the fourteen-year-old prince Alphonso, Isabella's other brother. However, when Alphonso died in 1468, these nobles switched their allegiance to Isabella.

Isabella, who was now seventeen years old, did not cooperate with the rebellious noblemen. Instead, she followed her own

Queen Isabella donates her jewels to Christopher Columbus before his grand voyage.

ed a number of suitors—including the one picked by Henry—and chose Ferdinand II, king of Sicily and heir to Aragon (a kingdom neighboring Castile). She saw in him the physical strength and training in war that she needed, but she also realized that he needed her allegiance at least as much as she needed his. Aragon was under attack from France, and Ferdinand would need the combined resources of Aragon and Castile to resist this pressure.

Knowing what Ferdinand faced, Isabella imposed on him a marriage agreement that would keep her power intact when she inherited the Castilian throne. He agreed to live in Castile and to provide her with military support, but he would not gain any authority of his own in Castile. In addition, any rights he did have would end when she died, so he could not inherit her kingdom. In 1474, when her half brother died, she became queen. During her thirty-year rule Isabella I ruthlessly enforced Catholicism, which she saw as the only true religion. She promoted education and the science of navigation; supported the textile, glassmaking, and leather industries; and stabilized the country politically. Under Isabella, Castile prospered. She is perhaps most famous for financing the Italian mariner Christopher Columbus in his attempt to reach Asia by sailing westward across the Atlantic in 1492, leading to the European discovery of the New World.

ideas about how to attain power. She declared her loyalty to Henry in exchange for a public declaration that she was his heir. She then set about finding a husband who would enable her to take control once she inherited the crown. She reject-

Making the Most of Her Influence

The wife of one French king and the mother of three more, Catherine de Médicis was, unlike Isabella, never queen in her own right, yet as queen mother she made the most of her influence. Also unlike Isabella, Catherine was driven not by a deep-seated belief in one true faith, but by a vision of religious tolerance and the peaceful coexistence of Catholics and Protestants.

Born into the rich and powerful Medici family in Florence, Italy, Catherine was orphaned before she was two months old and grew up under the guardianship of powerful relatives, two of whom were popes. When the city of Florence rebelled against Médicis control, the city leaders held Catherine hostage. Because she was a marriageable girl, she faced particular dangers. Realizing that the Médicis might form a powerful alliance by marrying her into another dominant family, the rebel leaders suggested placing the little girl in a brothel or having her raped by common soldiers. After such a disgrace, she would be worthless in the marriage market. The city leaders finally decided that she was too important a hostage for this treatment, but as historian Abel A. Alves says, "These brutal suggestions demonstrate the extent to which male political actors viewed her as a mere pawn."[66]

In her later life, Catherine emerged as much more than a pawn. At the age of fourteen she was married to the French duke of Orléans, who was also just fourteen and who later became King Henry II of France. The Venetian ambassador to France described the impact she had on the French court: "Although she is not beautiful, she has a certain wisdom and an extraordinary prudence; there is no doubt that she would be very capable of governing."[67] His words were prophetic, though it was some time before Catherine showed her abilities. Initially, she lived quietly, maintaining a polite relationship with Henry's mistress, Diane de Poitiers, and trying to fulfill her duty of producing heirs, sometimes resorting to cures such as wearing a magical amulet or drinking potions of rabbit's blood and sheep's urine. However, ten years passed before she had her first child. She would have nine more before Henry died of injuries suffered in a jousting accident in 1559.

Catherine had her first taste of power in 1552 when Henry, leaving to lead his troops in battle, appointed her regent in his absence. She resolved to learn the craft of government. "I assure you," she wrote to an aide, "I am going to be a past master at it; for from one hour to the next I study only this."[68]

Leading in the Role of Queen Mother

When she became queen mother after Henry's death, Catherine was ready to take a powerful role in French political life. Three of her sons—Francis II, Charles IX, and Henry III—became king in turn. Charles was only ten years old when he was crowned, and Catherine acted as his regent. This was a period of religious strife in France, with the Protestants (known as Huguenots) locked in conflict with the majority Catholic faction. Catherine herself, although she was a Catholic, was motivated not by religious zeal but by the need to rescue the country from an economic crisis. Seeing the Wars of Religion as costly to the nation, she tried to create a balance of power between the two sides, saying, "I hope it will be recognized that women are more inclined to conserve the kingdom than those who have put it in the condition in which it is." [69] This difficult task required all her political skill.

In September 1563 Catherine, who loved horses and introduced a new style of sidesaddle riding to France, had a serious accident when her horse fell on top of her. She developed a pain in her head that became so severe she could not move. She described the treatment: "A small opening was made in my head, near where the pain was worst, which caused such improvement that the pain was immediately assuaged." [70] But while she recovered there was no strong leadership, and an ambassa-

Family History of Defiant Women

During the Renaissance the Medici family gained a reputation for strong leadership. Lorenzo de Medici was famous for his political ability and for funding artists like Botticelli and Michelangelo. However, as Theodore K. Rabb explains in *Renaissance Lives,* his death left the family without clear leadership, and "it was primarily the women who held the family together." One of these decisive women was Clarice, aunt of Catherine de Médicis and one of the people who helped raise her. After Rome was sacked in 1527, most of the Medici family, includ-ing the current pope, were expelled from the city:

Clarice, however, refused to flee. She denounced her pusillanimous [cowardly] relatives, including the pope, as unworthy of their Medici ancestors, and encouraged the remaining men to leave with the ringing taunt: "The Medici Palace is not a stable for mules." Though they could depart with the family name, she said, she would stay on to defend the family honor. She was still scolding when a mob entered the palace, and drove her out.

Women of the Renaissance

dor from Florence wrote anxiously, "On the queen's life depends the salvation of this kingdom."[71] The queen did survive, and her wisdom and political skills helped guide the threatened French monarchy through wars and religious disputes.

"The Heart and Stomach of a King"

The English Renaissance is also known as the Elizabethan Age because of the profound influence of one queen, Elizabeth I. She became queen after the death of her half sister, Mary, and was determined to rule her own kingdom. Historian Pearl Hogrefe says that Elizabeth's "ambition to be great as a ruler was the greatest urge in her life."[72] Fulfilling this ambition meant resisting pressure to marry.

Even before Elizabeth became queen, Mary and her husband, Philip of Spain, hoped to seal an alliance with the Duke of Savoy by marrying Elizabeth off to him. But when Mary and Philip summoned Elizabeth from Hatfield House and announced their plan, she stubbornly refused the match. "Though she went back to Hatfield in disgrace," explains Hogrefe, "she was still mistress of herself and her future."[73]

As queen, Elizabeth remained determined to be her own mistress, although people everywhere—both in England and abroad—fully expected her to marry. Single Renaissance women had virtually no

Queen Elizabeth I of England refused to marry and ruled as a powerful monarch in her own right.

legal status, and queens were no exception, but Elizabeth gradually created for herself a role as unmarried female monarch. In the process, she had many suitors and sometimes engaged in long negotiations. The bargaining itself brought political advantages and allowed her to play foreign powers against one another. Elizabeth finally turned them all down and also declined to marry any of the men of her own court, although she may have truly loved her favorite adviser, Robert Dudley, Earl of Leicester.

To fulfill her role as an active queen, Elizabeth had to alter the Renaissance perception that a woman should be chaste, silent, and obedient. She remained chaste and was known as the Virgin Queen (the colony of Virginia was named in her honor), but she was neither silent nor obedient to any man. As she journeyed around England on her spectacular tours, she took every opportunity to make speeches, though public speaking was forbidden to most women. And while she drew on the political and diplomatic expertise of the men who advised her, she did not hand over authority to them but demanded that they obey her.

In 1588, when the Spanish Armada (an invading fleet of ships) was expected to attack, Elizabeth—against the advice of some counselors who feared for her safety—traveled to Tilbury where the English army was ready to resist an invasion. In a rousing speech to her troops, she defied the accepted view of a woman, claiming instead that she could fulfill every aspect of the role of king:

I know I have the body but of a weak and feeble woman; but I have the heart and stomach [courage] of a king, and of a king of England, too, and think foul scorn that Parma or Spain or any other prince of Europe should dare to invade the borders of my realm; to which, rather than any dishonor should grow by me, I myself will take up arms, I myself will be your general, judge, and rewarder of every one of your virtues in the field. [74]

Elizabeth's personal courage and political skill enabled her to create a unique role for herself. Her reign lasted for forty-five years, and when she died her chief adviser, Lord Burghley, said, "She was the wisest woman that ever was, for she understood the interests and dispositions of all the princes in her time, and was so perfect in the knowledge of her own realm, that no councillor she had could tell her anything she did not know before." [75]

Ruling a Troubled Kingdom

Mary Stuart, queen of Scotland, was nine years younger than her cousin Elizabeth. Mary came to the throne after her father's death, when she was just six days old. Although her mother acted as Mary's regent, many people despaired for the kingdom because the monarch was an infant—and, worse yet, a female. John Knox, a leader of the Protestant Reformation in Scotland, wrote that "all men lamented that the realm was left without a male to succeed." [76] Some of Mary's male relatives soon came forward to claim the throne, and the country plunged into political insecurity that was made worse by rivalry between Catholics and Protestants.

To strengthen ties with France, Mary's mother—who was herself French—negotiated a match between Mary and Francis, the eldest son of Henry II of France and Catherine de Médicis. At the age of five, Mary was sent to France and raised in the French court, and ten years later Mary and Francis were married. The marriage gave Francis the right to become king of Scotland if Mary should die before him. Many Scottish nobles were angry that Scotland was becoming dominated by France, and their opposition to Mary's rule deepened.

Just a year after their marriage, Francis inherited the French throne, and Mary became queen of France. However, Francis's reign lasted little more than a year. He died in 1560, and Mary saw that she had no future in France where her mother-in-law, Catherine de Médicis, dominated the court. Mary returned to Scotland, where

Secret Codes, Hidden Messages, and a Double Agent

During the period when she was under house arrest in Chartley Hall, England, Mary Queen of Scots communicated secretly with her supporters in code. Simon Singh, writing in *The Code Book,* describes how Mary's courier, Gilbert Gifford, delivered the encoded messages:

He had a rather cunning way of sneaking messages into Chartley Hall. He took the messages to a local brewer, who wrapped them in a leather packet, which was then hidden inside a hollow bung used to seal a barrel of beer. The brewer would deliver the barrel to Chartley Hall, whereupon one of Mary's servants would open the bung and take the contents to the Queen of Scots. The process worked equally well for getting messages out of Chartley Hall.

Unfortunately for Mary, this system was no match for the counterespionage of Elizabeth's spymaster, Sir Francis Walsingham, who persuaded Gifford to act as a double agent. Walsingham's men made copies of these messages and resealed the originals into the bungs. Walsingham's expert code breaker, Thomas Phelippes, deciphered the messages and thus discovered Mary's involvement in a plot to kill Elizabeth. Finally Elizabeth concluded that Mary must be executed.

she hoped to bring about a peaceful coexistence between Catholics and Protestants. In addition, she hoped to improve her relations with Elizabeth so that, as the English queen's nearest relative, Mary would be declared heir to the English throne.

Failed Marriages

Mary had difficulty establishing control over her troubled kingdom. Hoping that marriage would add to her authority, she

Mary Queen of Scots is shown in this French portrait.

considered a number of suitors. Both her beauty and her positions as queen of Scots and as claimant to the English throne made her an attractive match, and she considered offers from a number of European princes. However, her nobles were still nervous that a foreign marriage would mean foreign domination. Instead she married her cousin, Lord Darnley, who himself was a possible heir to the English throne. But even this marriage was unpopular, and it prompted a rebellion led by Mary's half brother. Riding at the head of her army, she drove the rebel forces across the border into England.

In 1566 Mary had a son (the future king of Scotland and England), but her marriage was not a success, and she had favorites who were thought to be her lovers. In 1567 Darnley was murdered. The house where he was staying was blown up one night when Mary was out, and Darnley's strangled body was found in the garden. Both Elizabeth I and Catherine de Médicis advised Mary to act swiftly to try suspects for the crime, but she ignored their advice, and rumors spread that she was an accomplice to the murder. The rumors increased when, months after Darnley's death, Mary married the Earl of Bothwell, one of the main suspects in the murder.

This marriage, too, was a failure. Mary herself was unhappy, and her nobles rebelled, promising that they would restore their loyalty if she abandoned Bothwell. But she refused, and many of her own troops deserted her. Bothwell finally fled to Denmark, where he was imprisoned. Still, the rebel lords captured Mary and locked her up in an island fortress. A year later she escaped to England and appealed to Elizabeth for sanctuary. But, nervous of the rebellious situation in neighboring Scotland, Elizabeth kept her cousin under house arrest.

Mary spent the remaining years of her life in English castles where she was well cared for but also closely watched. She never ceased to try to establish her rule and was suspected in a number of plots to escape, to seize the English throne, and to take back control of Scotland. Elizabeth's advisers warned of the danger of keeping Mary alive, but it was not until she was found to be involved in a plot against Elizabeth herself that the English queen agreed to the trial of her cousin on charges of treason. Mary was found guilty and expected to be executed, but Elizabeth hesitated. As Mary's biography in *Women in World History* suggests, Elizabeth was "perhaps fearful of the international repercussions of killing an anointed queen, and perhaps a little sympathetic to the cousin whom she had never met face to face."[77] Finally, though, Elizabeth agreed to the beheading. Mary's struggle to govern came to an end.

Accidents of birth and death led these outstanding women to positions of power on the thrones of England, Scotland, and Castile, and in the palaces of France. Their struggles and successes challenged the Renaissance view of a woman's capabilities and made an indelible mark on the history of Europe.

Chapter 5:
Women Rebels: Politicians to Pirates

❦

Most Renaissance women filled socially acceptable, subservient roles. A few rebellious women, however, seized opportunities to break from those roles and became famous for more unorthodox achievements. Some women worked within the royal courts to gain influence. Others who were born into powerful families followed the lead of their politically active male relatives rather than accepting the traditional role of a woman. A few women—pirates, soldiers, and criminals—took such a rebellious stance that they challenged the structure of Renaissance society.

Good Advice for the King of France

The Frenchwoman Diane de Poitiers gained a position of influence in the French court. She was married at the age of fifteen to a fifty-five-year-old man who soon went off to war, leaving Diane in charge of his castle and estate. When he was not fighting, Diane's husband, often accompanied by his wife, attended King Francis I. Diane was attractive, intelligent, and ener-

getic, and she made a favorable impression on the king and other courtiers.

The king's younger son, Henry, was especially attracted to Diane. After becoming heir to the throne at seventeen when his elder brother died, Henry turned to this well-informed, elegant woman for guidance and advice. Their relationship began as mentor and student, but they soon became lovers, despite the fact that Diane was twenty years older.

As mistress to the king (Henry inherited the throne in 1547), Diane was far more than a sexual partner. She and Henry spent many hours together—"at least eight hours a day"[78] according to one ambassador—hunting, riding, talking, and reading. One book they read together was Machiavelli's *The Prince,* a guide to acquiring and maintaining absolute power that influenced political thought throughout Renaissance Europe. Historian Claire Hsu Accomando describes the leadership qualities that Henry found helpful in Diane as well as the abilities that allowed her to exert her influence over him:

Having managed a large estate in the absence of her husband, Diane had acquired a sound practical sense, and Henry relied on her judgment and on her pragmatic approach. In addition, she knew how to obtain her wants through reason rather than caprice, diplomacy rather than coercion.[79]

Her role in the royal household extended to supervising the raising of Henry's chil-dren with his wife, Catherine de Médicis, and helping to arrange their marriages. Henry rewarded her with gifts of land and money and gave her the title Duchess of Valentinois.

Attending Queen Elizabeth's "Most Precious Person"

Another woman who created a role at court for herself was Mary Sidney. Her hus-band, Sir Henry Sidney, served Elizabeth I

This sixteenth-century painting shows a Renaissance woman who makes a living by cheating at cards.

A Close-Knit Group of Women at the Center of Power

Mary Sidney and Bess of Hardwick were members of a group of attendants who were more than simply servants and were with Queen Elizabeth night and day. In *The Life of Elizabeth I,* Alison Weir explains, "Like most male courtiers, the Queen's ladies were well-educated and well-read. Most studied, read the Bible or translated works by Latin or Greek authors."

Blanch Parry cared for Elizabeth when she was an infant, acted as her tutor, and stayed with the queen until her own death. Mary Radcliffe served at court for forty years, turning down several offers of marriage. Mary Hastings was terrified of being forced into a political marriage with the Russian czar Ivan the Terrible, so Elizabeth protected her by refusing permission for the marriage. When Margaret Radcliffe's twin brother was killed in battle, Elizabeth herself broke the news to the young woman.

Anne Russell, countess of Warwick, served the queen for many years. Her niece (quoted in *Sir Philip Sidney: Courtier Poet* by Katherine Duncan-Jones) described her as "being more beloved and in greater favour with the said Queen than any other woman in the kingdom." She was at Elizabeth's side at times of political tension and was with her when she died. Anne's sister-in-law, Mary Sidney, understood the cost of political errors: her brother, her sister-in-law (Lady Jane Grey), and her father were all executed by Mary Tudor.

as governor of Wales and as her lord deputy in Ireland. These positions took Sir Henry away from court and prevented him from engaging in the political jockeying necessary to promote his career.

Sidney turned to his wife, who spent much of her time at court, to help him gain the queen's notice. As Mendelson and Crawford explain, "Court ladies performed important functions for their families. They kept an ear out for news, and corresponded with distant kin."[80] Mary had even more importance. She was one of a group of women who had access to the queen. Although Elizabeth's public advisers were men (surrounding herself with men helped strengthen her authority as monarch), she spent many of her private hours with these women. Mary was intelligent and well educated, and she established a friendship with the queen. When Elizabeth contracted smallpox—an often fatal disease in the era before vaccination—Mary helped nurse her. Elizabeth survived the illness and did not even suffer the permanent scarring that often resulted. However, Mary caught the disease, and she was left with scars that destroyed her complexion. She was so self-conscious of this deformity that from then on she avoided appearing in public. As her husband wrote:

> When I went to Newhaven [Le Havre] I left her a full fair lady, in mine eyes at least the fairest, and when I returned I found her as foul a lady as the small-pox could make her, which she did take by continual attendance of her Majesty's most precious person . . . so as she lives solitarily.[81]

Mary worked on behalf of her husband, writing letters and maintaining the social and political ties that would help him fulfill his current position and rise to the next level. Biographer Duncan-Jones writes:

> Mary Sidney had to fight many of her husband's political battles for him, and, despite her scarred appearance, needed to maintain a frequent presence at Court. In a letter to his father in 1578 [Mary's son, Philip] Sidney paid tribute to the thoroughness and wisdom with which his mother was promoting the absent Sir Henry's interests, adding that "For mine own part, I have had only light from her."[82]

Preventing Treacherous Plots

Another Englishwoman who acquired power and wealth through her own efforts was Bess of Hardwick. Born in 1518 into a respectable but not wealthy family, she married for the first time at the age of fifteen. Her husband died two years later, and she used her small inheritance to support herself at court, where she showed an aptitude for handling the political and social

Bess of Hardwick became Queen Elizabeth's favorite lady-in-waiting.

complexities of court life. She married three more times, inheriting her husbands' property, so that by the end of her life she was very wealthy.

When Elizabeth I came to the throne, she made Bess a lady-in-waiting. Later Elizabeth said of Bess, "There is no lady in this land I better love and like." [83]

In 1568 Elizabeth gave Bess and her husband responsibility for housing Mary Stuart, queen of Scots, and her entourage of servants. Mary had been forced out of her kingdom by rebellious nobles and came to England for sanctuary. However, Elizabeth realized that Mary had hopes of obtaining the English throne as well as reclaiming Scotland and that the deposed queen would be the focus of treacherous plots. Consequently Elizabeth insisted that Mary be kept under house arrest, with her correspondence closely monitored. This supervision became Bess's responsibility, and it placed her in a position of unusual power in the relationship between the two queens.

A Life of Action in the Papal States

Caterina Sforza was one of a few Renaissance women who became both a political and a military leader. Born into the turbulent political life of the competing Italian city-states, Caterina was ten years old when she was betrothed to twenty-nine-year-old Girolamo Riario, a nephew of the pope. Although she was given the usual education for a girl, Caterina preferred horses and hunting to needlework and music, and she pursued a life of action.

The pope, struggling to bring the papal states of central Italy under control, granted territories to Girolamo, thus giving him the responsibility for defending them. He did so ruthlessly, acquiring a reputation for cruelty. Meanwhile Caterina took an interest in military affairs. Despite almost continuous pregnancies (she had nine children in twenty years), she commanded troops and, like her husband, enforced strict discipline.

The pope's death in 1484 brought disorder to Rome, with rival groups attempting to control the election of the successor. Girolamo was ordered by the church leaders to stay outside the city, but Caterina saw that their decree did not extend to her. Although she was seven months pregnant, she rode with her troops into Rome and seized the fortress of Castel Sant' Angelo. However, Girolamo and Caterina were soon forced to retreat to their own territories.

In 1487 Girolamo was left weakened by an illness, and Caterina took control of their estates. The fortress of Ravaldino, which was claimed by the previous owners, was a crucial stronghold, but the keeper of the castle refused to let Caterina in. She followed a ruthless strategy of conspiracy and assassination and ultimately took it back. She punished the leaders of

Preserving Her Beauty

Like many Renaissance women, Caterina Sforza collected recipes for medicines and other concoctions. As a woman in a position of power, she was especially interested in formulas that were useful in the cutthroat world of Italian politics. In the biography *Caterina Sforza: A Renaissance Virago,* Ernst Breisach says that her collection of recipes included instructions on how to alter the metallic content of coins, make invisible ink, and prepare a deadly poison. Caterina's famous beauty contributed to her powerful image:

Her natural blond hair gleamed in the sun after being rinsed with any of the lotions of nettleseed or of ivy leaves or of saffron, cinnabar, and sulphur. Her skin was a flawless white, with unwanted hair removed, protected from the sun and with chapped spots healed by the application of a salve made of oils, wax, chickenfat, and mastic [a paste of powdered lime]. The teeth stood straight in two lines, whitened by daily cleaning with a piece of cloth on which charcoaled rosemary stems or pulverized marble, coral cuttlebone, or mastic were spread. The mouth was then rinsed with a mouthful of good wine. Caterina's blue eyes took on a special sparkle after a washing with rosewater. Her prominent breasts were smoothed to satin texture by massages with a cream of which one ingredient was lard from a male pig.

a later plot with execution and had their heads displayed on poles at the gates of the town.

The following year Girolamo was stabbed to death, and Caterina's position was threatened. After sending a message for help to her family in Milan, the endangered woman barricaded herself and her children in her apartments. An angry mob broke in, however, and took them all prisoner. With the children as hostage, Caterina's captors allowed her to go to the fortress of Ravaldino and meet with its keeper. Once inside the stronghold, however, Caterina refused to submit to demands for surrender. Finally troops arrived from Milan, and Caterina—now twenty-five years old—recaptured her estates and was reunited with her children. Years later one observer described her as "still full of the devil and strong willed."[84]

Controlling the Pope's Affairs

Perhaps the best-known politically powerful woman of the Italian Renaissance was Lucrezia Borgia. Born the illegitimate daughter of a cardinal of the church, her early life was conventional. At that time, although priests were not permitted to marry, senior churchmen often openly had mistresses, and the children of bishops and cardinals were raised like princes and princesses. Thus Lucrezia, like the daughter of any powerful nobleman, was a highly valued marriage partner. One contemporary wrote that "she has a very beautiful face, bright laughing eyes and is erect of stature; she is delicate, modest, well learned, gracious, gay and very finely mannered." [85]

Her powerful father, who was elected pope in 1492, married Lucrezia off to a nobleman and then—when a different political alliance became important—he annulled that marriage and married her to a different one. However, he also saw that his daughter could be more than simply a means of creating political alliances. When she was eighteen, he made her regent over some of his territories. Two years later, when the pope traveled away from Rome, he left her in charge of his correspondence—a position that gave her control of much of his important business. Her husband, the Duke of Ferrara, also relied on her, leaving her to govern his territory for several years when he was at war. Lucrezia has often been depicted as a murderess who poisoned opponents of the Borgia family. Today, scholars recognize that she was caught up

Lucrezia Borgia was one of the most politically powerful women of Renaissance Italy.

in the violence of her time and place. By her contemporaries, Lucrezia was praised both for her abilities as a political leader and for creating a center of culture at her court, where she supported poets, painters, and performers.

Rebelling Against Society's Rules

Upper-class Renaissance women such as Diane de Poitiers, Mary Sidney, and Caterina Sforza could use their high position to influence politics and culture. Most lower-class women had to put all their energy into feeding their families, but desperation sometimes drove them to take actions that challenged the social order despite the lack of such assets.

Lower-class rebellion was fueled by necessity. For example, in the English city of Norwich in 1528 women rioted against rising grain prices. Other women defied laws that restricted their ability to make a profit in business. Anna Weylandin was a vendor in the city of Strasbourg who often clashed with the authorities. Wiesner describes the problems that developed in 1573, when Weylandin sought permission to sell herring [fish] from north Germany:

> This was granted despite the objections of the fishers' guild, but she was soon charged with refusing to sell this herring to people unless they also bought dried and salted cod from her. The following year she was charged with buying herring outside the city instead of at the public fish market, then selling it cheaper than the estab-lished price to undersell the other fishmongers and telling her customers not to say anything. She also got into the candle business the same year and was immediately charged with selling candles for less than the official price. [86]

Religious persecution also led women (as well as men) to challenge authority. One old woman helped incite an attack on Walter Raleigh (father of Sir Walter Raleigh, the Elizabethan courtier and colonist). She was walking to church with her rosary beads in her hands when Raleigh rode by on his horse. Seeing the beads, he asked her what they were for and reminded her—perhaps in an intimidating way—of the penalties that were then in force against Catholic worship. When she reached the church, she told her neighbors of what had happened, saying that Raleigh had threatened to burn their homes and seize their property if they continued Catholic practices. Historian Barrett Beer describes what happened:

> Walter Raleigh's words did not go unanswered, for a party of villagers set off in hot pursuit after him. The townspeople overtook him, abused him with insolent talk, and forced him to seek refuge in a chapel. . . . Raleigh might have been murdered had he not been rescued by mariners from Exmouth. [87]

Legendary Fighters

Some of the most colorful Renaissance rebels have become legendary characters. Their actions were recorded in songs and in pamphlets that were sold on the streets of their cities even in their own time. One woman, known as Long Meg of Westminster, was famous in London for standing up to thieves who picked on women because they seemed like easy targets. A story (retold by historian Joy Wiltenburg) tells of how, when Meg and her friends were attacked, she took on two thieves at once: "'Do your worst,' quoth [said] she. 'Now lasses, pray for me.' With that she buckled [fought] with these sturdy knaves and hurt one sore and beat down the other, [so] that they intreated [begged] her upon their knees to save their lives."[88]

She let the thieves go, on one condition: that they promise never again to attack a group that included a woman, children, or any poor or helpless people. Later, according to legend, Meg joined the army and fought for Henry VIII against France.

Another woman who became a legend was Mary Ambree, famous for her valor as a soldier. In 1584, the city of Ghent in the Netherlands was besieged by the Spanish, and Dutch and English volunteers came to the city's defense. Mary was one of these volunteers, and she became a captain in the army. Her courage was celebrated in numer-ous songs and stories. One song says that "for one of her own men, a score [twenty] killed she."[89]

Women Pirates

Shipping in general increased dramatically during the Renaissance, as England, Spain, and Portugal became naval powers and promoters of exploration for profit and conquest in the New World. In this age of exploration and empire building, vessels crossing the seas often carried—or were rumored to carry—valuable cargoes, and piracy became a constant threat.

Piracy took a number of forms. When a ship wrecked offshore, local people often rushed to take advantage of the accident by looting the cargo that washed ashore. Sometimes shore folk known as wreckers would deliberately cause shipwrecks by lighting lamps and fires to confuse navigators into running aground, and then plunder the damaged vessels. In contrast, seagoing pirates would try to take over a ship without damaging it so that they gained the vessel as well as its cargo. Although piracy of all kinds was generally illegal, Renaissance governments would sometimes encourage pirates to attack the ships of enemy countries. The sailors who manned pirate ships and attacked other vessels were almost all men, but some women also took part in this dangerous way of life.

The Killigrew family, which included several pirates, lived in a castle overlooking the busy harbor of Falmouth in southwest Britain. Once the elderly Lady Killigrew seized an opportunity to steal a ship and its cargo. In January 1582 a ship entered Falmouth harbor to escape a storm. The captain and master came ashore, and Lady Killigrew—a hospitable woman in her sixties—invited them into the castle to shelter from the storm. Assuring the two men that their ship would be safe, Lady

This illustration depicts a typical sailing vessel of the sixteenth century. Piracy became a common threat in the Renaissance as shipping increased dramatically.

Killigrew suggested that they wait out the storm in a nearby guest house. But when the storm had passed, the men emerged to find no sign of their ship in the harbor. As the storm was dying down, Lady Killigrew and her pirates had attacked the ship in the dark and killed all the crew. According to the German writers Ulrike Klausmann, Marion Meinzerin, and Gabriel Kuhn, "With fully-laden boats, the lady and two of her gang returned to the castle, where they dragged the rolls of cloth and kegs into a hiding-place. The other pirates disappeared into the dark with the ship." [90]

"Director of Thieves and Murderers at Sea"

The most famous woman pirate of the Renaissance was Grace O'Malley, a clan leader from the west of Ireland. The O'Malley clan controlled key shipping and fishing areas, levying tolls and selling fish-

"Roaring Her Men into Action"

Historian Anne Chambers has studied the historical accounts and the folklore surrounding the life of the legendary woman pirate Grace O'Malley (whom she calls Granuaile, the Irish language version of her name). In *Bold in Her Breeches: Women Pirates Across the Ages*, edited by Jo Stanley, Chambers writes:

Folklore maintains that Granuaile married Richard [Bourke] for "one year certain" and that if after that period either party wished to withdraw they were free to do so. . . . Under Brehon law, the ancient, native law of Gaelic Ireland, divorce was permitted and was the right of either party. . . .

When Granuaile's marriage to Richard Bourke reached a year's duration, she installed her men in [Bourke's] Rockfleet Castle, locked the castle against him and shouted from the ramparts "Richard Bourke I dismiss you," thereby divorcing herself of a husband and obtaining a fine castle in lieu of her dowry. But Granuaile and Richard were reunited and their son born at sea. The day after his birth, her ship was attacked by an Algerian corsair. According to stories, as the battle raged on deck, her captain came below where she lay with her new-born son and begged for help. "May you be seven times worse off this day twelve months, who cannot do without me for one day," she upbraided him and stormed on deck. The Algerian pirates allegedly stood transfixed at the dishevelled female apparition. Roaring her men into action, she led them to victory.

ing rights. Their castles—strategically located at coastal inlets—provided safe havens for their small fleet of ships and its sailors. In addition to enforcing the clan's control over shipping and fishing, this fleet attacked foreign vessels, overcoming their crews and stealing their cargoes.

Grace defied tradition and law to take control of her father's fleet. Her skill as a sailor and navigator meant she could use her ships effectively, despite the dangerous reefs and currents in her territory. She also had great stamina and was able to withstand the harsh conditions on board ship, where there was no escaping the cold and wet. Grace was a dynamic leader, and, as historian Anne Chambers suggests, she must have had "some charisma that forged such a lasting bond between her and her men that they were willing to be led by a woman."[91]

Fearing that Spain would use Ireland as a "back door" into mainland Britain, Elizabeth I attempted to bring the island under British rule. Her officers were astonished when they met the powerful, warlike Grace.

One Englishman described her as a "woman who overstepped the part of womanhood"[92]; another called her the "great spoiler and chief commander and director of thieves and murderers at sea."[93] Grace's negotiations with the English eventually led to a meeting with Elizabeth. Grace sailed to Greenwich, near London, and the two women—who differed greatly in lifestyle, but shared the achievement of having created a powerful role in a male-dominated society—held talks. No records of their conversation exist, but after the meeting Elizabeth gave orders for the release of Grace's son, who was in English custody.

These political leaders, rebels, and pirates—so different in their backgrounds and life histories—shared one characteristic: They broke the bounds of Renaissance womanhood. Forced by desperate circumstances or encouraged by unusual opportunities, and drawing upon extraordinary ability and determination, they defied society's expectations of women's subordination and achieved unconventional prominence.

Chapter 6:
Women Scholars and Scientists

The Renaissance intellectual movement called humanism placed a high value on scholarship, which in this age meant rediscovering and studying the Latin and Greek classic texts and increasing the body of scientific knowledge. Indeed, great advances in learning are one of the hallmarks of the Renaissance era. Scholarly education was rarely available to girls, however, because education was seen as a way to mold political leaders, and no Renaissance woman was expected to assume a leadership role. It is true that Queen Elizabeth and her circle were famous for their scholarly interests and achievements, but, as scholar Jacqueline Eales has pointed out, "The learned women of the Tudor court numbered no more than fifteen high-profile individuals and, although educational opportunities were opening for men, these remained closed for women."[94]

Further limiting girls' educational opportunities were the era's increasing restrictions on women's entering the learned professions such as law and medi-cine. For example, no woman is known to have practiced as a physician in Frankfurt after 1479 (as the Middle Ages drew to a close), although this city had been famous in medieval times for its female eye specialists. Some wealthy Renaissance mothers maintained a family tradition of scholarly education for their daughters—the era's version of home schooling—but only exceptional women gained enough education to become known to history as a scholar or scientist.

In general, Renaissance education for girls was nonexistent or extended only to what was thought necessary for running a household. Historian King writes:

Poor women, like poor men, received no formal education whatsoever, although many men and some women were trained in certain crafts. Middle- and upper-class women were initiated in a particular female culture, however, in which they were taught to perform household functions and pursued a regimen stressing needlework and spinning, silence and obedience. Reading was useful, but should be limited to good books. . . . The goals of education for these women were twofold: first, to guide the young woman to develop those traits of character most suited to patriarchal marriages; second, to train her in those skills most useful in the domestic economy.[95]

Directly or indirectly, governments strove to channel girls' education along safe pathways designed to lead them into their intended roles as Good Wives. A contest held by the city council of Memmingen, beginning in 1587, reinforced this ideal. The city awarded a prize to a girl student, who would be called "the queen." She was selected based on how well she learned the subjects then regarded as the principal ones suitable for a female: the basic religious information outlined in the catechism (a set of questions and answers), clear handwriting, and the personal attributes of modesty and obedience.

Approved Studies for Women

Even when women did get a humanist education, they often failed to receive the respect that such an achievement would bring to a man. During the Renaissance, only a very few men and boys received a humanist education, and almost no girls and women were able to master this new approach to scholarship. The few women who did manage to become humanist scholars were typically ignored, or given scant respect in comparison with the high praise accorded to men with similar scholarly achievements.

These limitations on women's scholarship had societal sources—and far-reaching consequences. The humanist scholar Leonardo Bruni outlined a broad curriculum for use in tutoring young noblewoman

A noblewoman studies a religious book in this sixteenth-century painting.

Battista Montefeltro. He included Latin works of history, moral philosophy, and poetry such as men of the time studied, but with the exception of rhetoric (public speaking). He feared that study of rhetoric would "consume" Battista's "powers" and argued that, as a woman, she would never need debating skills. In fact, Bruni argued, a woman who tried to go into the forum (arena for debate) and express her thoughts in public might be considered mentally ill and imprisoned. "If she should gesture energetically with her arms as she spoke and shout with violent emphasis, she would probably be thought mad and put under restraint. The contests of the forum, like those of warfare and battle, are the sphere of men." [96]

The dangers from which Bruni wished to protect Battista were quite real. The Renaissance fear of educated, articulate women is reflected in the fate of the Dutchwoman Elizabeth Dirks. The wife of persecuted religious leader Menno Simons (after whom the Mennonite Church is named), Dirks was captured in

A Curriculum for Girls

As Moira Ferguson points out in *First Feminists: British Women Writers 1578–1799,* "Bathsua Makin was the first Englishwoman to recommend a systematic program of advanced education for females." Makin's students would spend half their time learning "works of all sorts, dancing, music, singing, writing, and keeping accounts."

The other half [of the students' time] to be employed in gaining the Latin and French tongues. And those that please may learn Greek and Hebrew, the Italian and Spanish, in all which this gentlewoman [Makin] has a competent knowledge.

Gentlewomen of eight or nine years old, that can read well, may be instruct-ed in a year or two (according to their parts) in the Latin and French tongues, by such plain and short rules, accompanied to the grammar of the English tongue, that they may easily keep [remember] what they have learned, and recover what they shall lose, as those that learn music by notes. Those that will bestow longer time may learn the other languages, afore-mentioned, as they please.

Repositories also for visibles shall be prepared, by which, from beholding the things, gentlewomen may learn the names, natures, values, and use of herbs, shrubs, trees, mineral juices, metals, and stones.

Women of the Renaissance

Spinning wheels whir as women turn wool into yarn. Many Renaissance women learned to spin wool.

1549 by men who also searched their home. When he found a Latin Bible there, one of the captors called out, "We've got the right one. We've caught the teacher." They imprisoned Dirks and interrogated her. She answered by quoting verses from the Bible. Outraged by this evidence of unacceptable learning—and by her ability to debate—her interrogators responded, "Now we see you are a teacher because you make yourself equal to Christ."[97] To punish this heresy, they tied her in a sack and drowned her.

Winning Honor Through Study

Across Europe some women were determined to break out of their restricted roles and participate in the exciting discoveries of Renaissance scholarship. They wanted to share the honor accorded to men, who often won praise for their learning. One of these women was Louise Labé of Lyon, who was known for taking actions in opposition to society's expectations. Raised as a cordière, or rope maker, she married a publisher and began writing poetry and expressing her views in public. Labé also wore armor when attending tournaments, though the story that she would actually mount a horse and compete against armed knights in the jousting matches is now thought to be a myth. Labé wrote to her friend Mademoiselle Clémence de Bourges,

Since the time has come when men's harsh laws no longer prevent women from applying themselves to the arts and sciences, I believe that those of us with the ability to do so should employ it in study of this noble freedom which our sex has so long desired; and thereby show men how they have wronged us by depriving us of the benefits and honor that we might have enjoyed from study.

And if any of us excel to that degree that she can express her thoughts in writing, let her do so proudly and not resist the glory that she will win, greater than that won by necklaces, rings and fine fashions. For these are ours only because we have used them, but the honor which we win through study is truly ours. [98]

Among the women who sought fame as scholars were Italian sisters Isotta and Ginevra Nogarola of Verona. Their widowed mother had hired a tutor to give her daughters a thorough humanist education, and both became famous in their teens, exchanging public letters with male scholars and other important men. At age twenty-one, Ginevra married and ceased her studies, but Isotta was determined to continue. She rejected marriage and remained in a "book-lined cell" in her mother's house. Today Nogarola is best known not for her scholarly writings but for an exchange of letters that took place in 1437. One of her correspondents, Guarino Veronese, failed to reply to one of Nogarola's public letters, causing the women of Verona to mock her publicly. In her second letter to Guarino, Nogarola wrote:

There are already so many women in the world! Why then was I born a woman, to be scorned by men in words and deeds? I ask myself this question in solitude. I do not dare ask it of you, who have made me the butt of everyone's jokes. Your unfairness in not writing to me has caused me so much suffering that there could be no greater suffering. . . . You might have cared more for me if I had never been born. For they jeer at me throughout the city, the women mock me. I cannot find a quiet stable to hide in, and the donkeys [women] tear me with their teeth, the oxen [men] with their horns. [99]

Guarino did reply to this letter, acknowledging Nogarola's learning but also criticizing her, saying, "You seem so humbled, so abject, and so truly a woman, that you demonstrate none of the estimable qualities that I thought you possessed." He advised her, instead, to create "a man within the woman and face this abuse bravely, though your sex taunts you."[100] Unable or unwilling to take this advice, Nogarola abandoned her effort to achieve fame and spent the rest of her life isolated in her "cell," focusing her studies on religious topics.

Winning Fame as an Orator

A generation later, Cassandra Fedele achieved widespread admiration for her learning, having mastered Latin at age twelve, and also studying Greek, history, philosophy, sacred studies, and rhetoric. Fedele's study of public speaking enabled her to make orations before the doge (political leader) of Venice and achieve fame that reached across national borders and led to political consequences: "When

More than "A Finer Sort of Cattle"

Bathsua Makin was one of the most learned women of her time. Yet when she was introduced to King James "for an English rarity, because she could speak and write pure Latin, Greek and Hebrew, the king asked, 'But can she spin?'" (quoted in Frances Teague, *Bathsua Makin, Woman of Learning*). In 1673, Makin established a school for girls and wrote *An Essay to Revive the Ancient Education of Gentlewomen* to explain why girls should be taught more than just how to spin:

Had God intended women only as a finer sort of cattle, he would not have made them reasonable [capable of reason]. Brutes, a few degrees higher than drills [mandrills, or baboons] or monkeys . . . might have better fitted [suited] some men's lust, pride, and pleasure, especially those that desire to keep them [women] ignorant to be tyrannized over. . . .

Persons of competent parts [abilities] . . . may and ought to be improved in more polite learning, in religion, arts, and the knowledge of things, in tongues also . . . rather than to spend the over-plus of their time of their youth in making points for bravery [braiding their hair in showy styles], in dressing and trimming themselves like Bartholomew babies [brightly dressed dolls equivalent to today's Barbie dolls], in painting and dancing, in making flowers of colored straw, and building houses of stained [colored] paper, and suchlike vanities.

Queen Isabella of Aragon invited Fedele to join her court, the young woman's decision to leave her fatherland was countermanded by the Venetian Senate, which issued a decree forbidding so great an asset to leave Venice."[101]

Unlike Nogarola, Fedele did marry, but she had no children. She was left destitute when her husband died after losing all of his property in a shipwreck. Fedele appealed to Pope Paul III for help and was made prioress of an orphanage. While in this position she appears to have been able to continue her classical studies: In 1556, only two years before her death at the age of ninety-three, Fedele delivered a Latin oration before the queen of Poland on the occasion of her visit to Venice.

Laura Cereta of Brescia, Italy, the daughter of a physician, was widowed at seventeen. Defiant by nature, she insisted on reading classical literature and studying philosophy and mathematics. However, Cereta met so much social opposition that she was not able to continue her studies. In 1488, she did manage to publish one outspoken letter to the men who opposed education for women:

> My ears are wearied by your carping. You . . . lament that I am said to possess as fine a mind as nature ever bestowed upon the most learned men. You seem to think that so learned a woman has scarcely before been seen in the world. You are wrong on both counts. . . . I would have been silent, believe me, if that savage old enmity of yours had attacked me alone. . . . But I cannot tolerate your having attacked my entire sex. For this reason my thirsty soul seeks revenge, my sleeping pen is aroused to literary struggle, raging anger stirs mental passions long chained by silence.[102]

Scholarly Leadership

Marguerite d'Angoulême, a member of the French nobility, was known as "the pearl of princesses."[103] She was another Renaissance woman scholar whose widowed mother, Louise de Savoie, believed in education. With her brother (who would become François I, king of France), Marguerite was tutored in all elements of humanist culture. She grew up to be an important figure in her brother's court and, when she became queen of Navarre, she created a lively intellectual environment in her own court. Anne Boleyn, later to marry King Henry VIII of England and become the mother of Queen Elizabeth, was part of Marguerite's court, and Erasmus, the leading humanist thinker, was her friend. Like her mother, Marguerite encouraged education; she persuaded the king to support humanist learning in the universities.

Today Marguerite's sponsorship of scholars and learning is regarded as more

Marguerite d'Angoulême (standing, left) fostered a lively intellectual environment in her court as queen of Navarre.

significant than her writing, which includes poetry, plays, devotional literature, and a series of stories, the *Heptameron*. Marguerite's writing was much appreciated in her own day, however, and Queen Elizabeth valued some of her poems enough to translate them from French into English. Marguerite also took a leadership role in the religious controversies that were transforming French society. Even though she never officially broke with the Catholic Church, she was influential in Reformation circles, at one time offering Etienne Dolet, husband of Lyon printer Louise Giraud, protection from religious persecution. Marguerite's nephew, Henri II of France, said of her, "If it were not for my aunt Margaret I should doubt the existence of such a thing as genuine goodness on the earth." [104]

"My Book Has Been So Much My Pleasure"

In *Lady Jane Grey* biographer Hester W. Chapman describes the young noblewoman's love of learning and recounts a conversation between Jane and Roger Ascham, a humanist scholar and tutor to the future Queen Elizabeth. Ascham, who believed that learning should be easy and agreeable, was impressed by Jane's account of the comfort she derived from her reading:

One of the greatest benefits that ever God gave me is that He sent me, with sharp, severe parents, so gentle a schoolmaster. When I am in presence of either father or mother, whether I speak, keep silence, sit, stand or go, eat, drink, be merry or sad, be sewing, playing, dancing or doing anything else, I must do it, as it were, in such weight, measure or number, even as perfectly as God made the world—or else I am so sharply taunted, so cruelly threatened, yea, presented sometimes with pinches, nips and bobs [blows] and other ways—which I will not name for the honor I bear them—so without measure misordered, *that I think myself in hell*—till the time comes when I must go to Mr Aylmer, who teaches me so gently, so pleasantly, with such fair allurements to learning, that I think the time nothing while I am with him.

And when I am called from him, I fall on weeping, because whatever I do else but learning is full of great trouble, and whole misliking unto me. And thus my book has been so much my pleasure, and brings daily to me more pleasure—and more—that in respect of it, all other pleasures, in very deed, be but trifles and troubles to me.

"Natural Philosophy" Becomes Science

In the early years of the Renaissance, scholars did not distinguish between philosophy and science, and the term "natural philosophy" was applied to all branches of what today is called science. Only gradually did people move away from a reliance on classical works by philosophers like Plato and Aristotle to develop ideas based on observation and experiment, as scientists do today, and the natural philosophers of the Renaissance world were predominantly men. Relatively few Renaissance women were able to make their mark as scientists, though some made significant contributions to scientific knowledge and others assisted better-known relatives in their work.

Whether they had a formal education or not, women's daily responsibilities required them to have knowledge of many technological processes, such as dyeing, that involved what today would be seen as scientific principles. As Renaissance educator Bathsua Makin pointed out, "To buy wool and flax, to dye [them] scarlet and purple, requires skill in natural philosophy."[105] Historian Lynette Hunter explains that in Renaissance times, everyday items such as soap, polish, toothpaste, and glue all had to be made in the household: "One case in point is ink. I know of no receipt [recipe] book or manuscript without its recipe for ink. Without it, of course, neither the book nor the manuscript would exist, yet it is not an easy thing to get that balance of dense blackness with the essential quality of quick drying."[106]

Renaissance women and men were interested in many different areas of learning, and whether the term "scientist" could be applied to a given individual often depends on the accidents of history. Anna Sophia of Denmark, wife of August I of Saxony, made her mark as a botanist. Like so many other Renaissance women, she raised medicinal herbs. The apothecary shop she established would survive for three hundred years—well into modern times. Tarquinia Molza was a polymath (a scholar knowledgeable in many areas) and also a musician. She is known for the recognition she received: the Senate of Rome made her a citizen of the city and gave her the right to transmit this honor to her descendants. Catherine de Parthenay, a French noblewoman, was tutored by excellent mathematicians and grew up to be a philosopher

Anna Sophia of Denmark established an apothecary shop that thrived for three hundred years.

and mathematician. When she became princess of Rohan, however, she turned her interests to classical literature, creating translations of works concerning the ideas of the ancient Greek philosopher Socrates.

Sophia Brahe was a sister of the Danish astronomer Tycho Brahe. Her education introduced her to classical literature, astrology (which was then little different from the science of astronomy), and alchemy. Tycho gained fame for making astronomical observations and calculating the lunar eclipse that occurred on December 8, 1573. His work would lead to recognition later in this era that the earth is not the center of the universe, as most people had believed. It would be inaccurate to describe Sophia Brahe as an astronomer herself. Yet Tycho's first biographer, Renaissance mathematician Pierre Gassendi, wrote of her, "She had been exposed to mathematics, and not only did she love astronomy but she was especially ready to engage in these exciting studies."[107]

Treating Body, Mind, and Soul

Oliva Sabuca of Alcaraz, Spain, grew up in a family of pharmacists. She achieved a legendary reputation in the sixteenth century and was mentioned in the works of two of Spain's greatest writers, Miguel de Cervantes and Lope de Vega. Yet the authorities of the Catholic Church almost succeeded in destroying all copies of her great work, a treatise on mental states titled *A New Philosophy of the Nature of Man, Not Known or Achieved by the Ancient Philosophers, Which Will Improve Human Life and Health*. Two copies survived, however, and the book was reprinted in the following century. Scholars Maria Vintro and Mary Ellen Waithe note that Sabuca dealt with "taboo physiological topics," pointing out that men also suffered from "hysteria," previously seen as a female condition and evidence of women's inferiority to men.[108]

Sabuca's ideas represented new thoughts: her belief that feelings such as fear, anger, shame, and compassion stimulated the brain to make secretions that could damage one's health. She said that the human body is like an "upside-down tree," with the brain like a "root" that controls the trunk and limbs, that is, the person's body, arms, and legs. Sabuca believed that a "nervous sap" of fluids related to one's mind and emotions influences all bodily processes. As Vintro and Waithe summarize Sabuca's work:

> Thus, psychological conditions (enthusiasm, interest, etc.) and moral virtues (love, hope, etc.) can positively affect physical health, and contribute to human growth and development. Conversely, negative psychological conditions (depression, sadness, etc.) and moral vices (hate, greed, etc.) negatively affect health, and contribute from disease to physical disorders. . . .

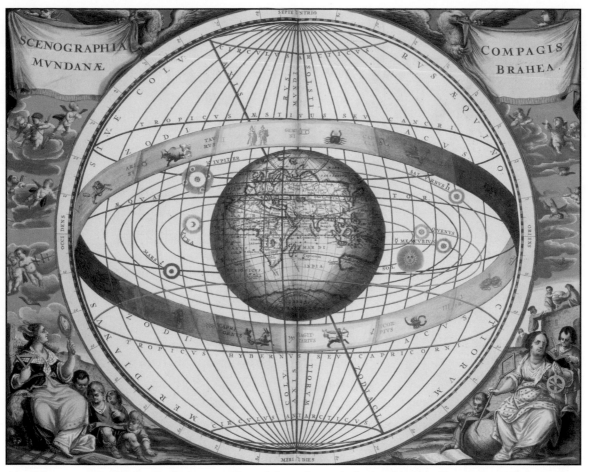

Danish astronomer Tycho Brahe's conception of the universe is depicted in this illustration. Tycho's sister Sophia took a keen interest in his astronomical observations.

Her philosophy of medicine is grounded in the avoidance of unnecessary disease, the living of a normal, healthy life, and reaching a peaceful, natural death. She urged physicians to treat the whole person: body, mind and soul, in unison.[109]

As the achievements of Sabuca and Brahe demonstrate, the contributions of Renaissance women to scholarship and sci-ence are impressive in their range, creativity, and scope. Rising above the harsh restrictions imposed on them, countless other women also sought knowledge by studying the works of ancient authors and by drawing conclusions from observations and experiments. Determined to learn as much as they could and to contribute to the growth of human understanding, these women played an often unrecognized role in the development of modern science.

Chapter 7:
Women Writers

In Renaissance culture, a writer was viewed as a type of public speaker, and thus women were generally excluded from this role. The great works of the Renaissance such as Machiavelli's *The Prince* and Castiglione's *The Courtier* were about politics and leadership—areas of life that were not open to most women. Poetry—although it was often about women—was mostly written by men, and most plays were not only written but also acted by men, with boys taking the parts of women. Even so, a number of Renaissance women created lasting literary works.

Translating the Words of Men

One way that women could find a place as writers and have their work published was by translating the works of male authors. As Margaret P. Hannay explains in her book about the English writer Mary Herbert, Countess of Pembroke, "Translation was one of the most common ways of evading censorship, and one extensively practiced by women, who were usually denied original public discourse [expression]." [110] Mary Her-

bert translated a number of works, including some of the psalms found in the Bible.

Mary Herbert was named for her mother, Mary Sidney, the notable friend and attendant of Queen Elizabeth I. Herbert herself became an attendant to the queen at the age of fifteen, when she married the Earl of Pembroke. Having been raised in a politically active family, Herbert was interested in the political topics that were discussed at the time. Through her translations, she managed to take part in these discussions.

Herbert hoped that the group of countries known as the Protestant alliance would prevail over Catholic Europe. She promoted the Protestant cause by translating the work of a French Protestant, Philippe de Mornay, and two plays by French dramatist Robert Garnier. As Hannay explains, her translations could even be read as criticisms of the queen and a warning to her of possible unrest:

The two dramas translated and sponsored by Mary Sidney emphasize political themes. Written during the 1590s, when the [Protestant] alliance saw Elizabeth's dalliance [flirtation] with [the Earl of] Essex as a threat to military intervention for the Protestant cause on the Continent, [the two plays] *Antonius* and *Cleopatra* stress the dangers of privileging private passion over public duty and warn of civil tumult. [111]

Had she confronted Elizabeth directly, Herbert would have risked banishment from the royal court—or worse punishment. But by translating works that held these powerful political messages, she was able to make her point safely.

Strength and Comfort for a Queen

Queen Elizabeth herself, a highly educated woman fluent in several languages, wrote poetry and translated the works of some Roman and Italian poets, though she never published her work. One work, *The Consolation of Philosophy* by the Roman poet and philosopher Boethius, seemed to appeal particularly to Elizabeth, perhaps because its consoling verses were a pleasant change from the rivalries of the royal court and the tensions of international politics, and she seemed to take strength and comfort from it. She translated this long work in just twelve days, working at it for two hours a day. Her secretary was

so impressed by her speed in accomplishing the task that he calculated the total hours spent on the project: "Accounting two hours bestowed every day, the computation falleth out that in twenty-four hours Your Majesty began and ended your translation." [112]

Elizabeth also found strength and comfort in her faith, and among her surviving writings are prayers, such as this one in which she asks for God's protection against

By translating French works about leadership, Mary Herbert expressed her own criticism of Queen Elizabeth with impunity.

traitors: "Grant, Oh God, that the wicked may have no power to hurt or betray me; neither suffer [permit] any such treason and wickedness to proceed against me. For thou, Oh God, canst mollify [soften] all such tyrannous hearts, and disappoint all such cruel purposes."[113]

Recording Family History

Philippe de Mornay, the French Protestant whose writing Mary Herbert translated into English, was married to a noblewoman named Charlotte Arbaleste. The religious tensions that divided Renaissance France affected Arbaleste personally: Her father became a Protestant in the 1560s, but her mother remained a Catholic. Arbaleste herself embraced the Reformed cause; her first husband was a Huguenot who was killed in the religious wars, leaving her with a five-month-old daughter. Some seven years later she met and married Mornay. Natalie Zemon Davis describes how Arbaleste dedicated herself to helping him in his work for the Protestant movement:

Charlotte was completely caught up in his work in France and abroad for the Reformed cause, sometimes helped

Escaping a Massacre

Charlotte Arbaleste was in Paris on August 24, 1572, when the St. Bartholomew's Day massacre began. This outbreak of mob violence led to the deaths of about seventy thousand Huguenots.

Being the daughter and widow of well-known Protestants, Charlotte was in grave danger, so she hid at the top of a friend's house with a servant, leaving her two-year-old daughter with the family below. In her memoir (*A Huguenot Family in the XVI Century*, translated by Lucy Crump), Charlotte described what happened:

While I was in this hollow above the attic I heard the most terrible cries from men, women and children who were being murdered in the streets, and having left my child below I fell into the greatest perplexity and almost despair so that, had I not feared God's wrath, I would far sooner have flung myself down than have fallen into the hands of the mob, or have seen my child massacred before my eyes.

Fortunately a servant girl escaped with the child to a safer place. Charlotte herself spent ten more days in hiding in the homes of friends and former servants. She eventually escaped from Paris by disguising herself as a servant.

him check references for his writings or found him a printer, but more often was kept at home by her pregnancies and ill health. She was informed of his doings by oral accounts; by his letters to her, often in code; and by an archive she established by dispatches and letters. [114]

Arbaleste's own life as a writer began in 1584 when she embarked on writing a memoir of her husband's life. The reason she wrote was to share with their son the remarkable story of faith and courage that made his father famous across Europe. In 1595, when the sixteen-year-old boy left home for the first time, she gave him what she had written so far. She would go on writing, however, for another ten years, stopping when her son was killed in battle.

Although Arbaleste's writing was primarily an account of her husband's life, she nonetheless described some events in her own life before she met Mornay. Depicting the bad situation she found herself in after the death of her first husband, Jean de Feuqueres, she conveys an impression of her own strong-mindedness as well as her faith in God:

I was nineteen years old, in deep trouble, away from my native land [Paris] and from all means of livelihood and harassed with an infinite amount of business. While at Sedan [in northeast France] I learnt of my father's death . . . , of a sister's death who was just about to be married and of my father-in-law's death as well. Such little property as I possessed had been seized on account of all the troubles; and I never saw a farthing [one-fourth of a penny] of M. de Feuqueres' fortune. But God raised me up friends, and helped me through all my troubles. [115]

Despite frequent illness, Arbaleste strove to be a good wife to Mornay, supporting his work for the Protestant movement. She describes how, in difficult circumstances, she managed their affairs without worrying her husband, and how she stayed in the background of his public life. However, in her writing she allows her own achievements to appear and lets her son see that his parents were partners in their courageous and eventful life.

Voicing the Fears of Women

While Arbaleste expressed herself through recording her family's history, other women chose to write poetry. One prolific poet was Vittoria Colonna, an Italian woman of deep faith who was active in the movement to reform the Catholic Church. Like most women writers of the time, she did not publish her writing, since women were expected to avoid public

Vittoria Colonna was a prolific poet who wrote love sonnets and religious poems.

He died of wounds he sustained in the war's final battle.

Most of Colonna's poetry was written after Pescara's death, when she retired to a convent. However, one poem survives from her married years. In it she voices the fears of women left behind when men go to war:

> Your uncertain enterprises do not
>   hurt you;
> But we who wait, mournfully
>   grieving,
> Are wounded by doubt and by fear.
> You men, driven by rage, consider-
>   ing nothing
> But your honor, commonly go off,
>   shouting,
> With great fury, to confront danger.
> We remain, with fear in our heart
>   and
> Grief on our brow for you; sister
>   longs
> For brother, wife for husband,
>   mother for son.[116]

Describing a Woman's Life

In contrast to the young wife's perspective given in Colonna's poem, the poetry of Englishwoman Martha Moulsworth reflects the views of a mature woman. Writing on her fifty-fifth birthday, Moulsworth looks back on her life, describing her experiences and expressing her wishes.

She recalls that her father brought her up "in godly piety" and that he provided

attention. Instead she circulated her poems—which number at least 390—among friends. Two collections of her poetry were printed during her lifetime, but without her permission.

At the age of seventeen, Colonna was married to the marquis of Pescara, but after only about one year together he left their home in Naples to take part in the war against France. The fighting continued for fifteen years, so Pescara was rarely home.

Women of the Renaissance

her with an education that was unusual for women at the time. Making the point that the Muses—the mythical figures thought to inspire learning and art—are depicted as women, Moulsworth suggests that women should be educated, and she even imagines what it would be like if there were a university for women:

Beyond my sex and kind
He [her father] did with learning
    Latin deck [adorn] my mind

And why not so? The muses female
    are
And therefore of us females take
    some care.
Two universities we have of men.
Oh that we had but one of women;
    then
Oh then that would in wit [intelli-
    gence], and tongues [languages]
    surpass
All art of men that is, or ever
    was. [117]

"Give to Women All Due Recognition"

Many of Vittoria Colonna's poems were inspired by her deeply held Christian faith. In this example (translated in *Women Writers of the Renaissance and Reformation*, edited by Katharina M. Wilson), Vittoria depicts a scene from the Bible, where, after the crucifixion of Jesus, Mary Magdalene visited his tomb while the male disciples were too afraid to do so.

Seized in her sadness by that great
    desire
Which banishes all fear, this beautiful
    woman,
All alone, by night, helpless, humble,
    pure,
And armed only with a living, burning
    hope,

Entered the sepulcher and wept and
    lamented;
Ignoring the angels, caring nothing for
    herself,
She fell at the feet of the Lord, secure,
For her heart, aflame with love, feared
    nothing.

And the men, chosen to share so many
    graces,
Though strong, were shut up together
    in fear;
The true Light seemed to them only a
    shadow.
If, then, the true is not a friend to the
    false,
We must give to women all due
    recognition
For having a more loving and more
    constant heart.

Moulsworth was married and widowed three times. Conscious that many women of her time were married to men who neglected or abused them, she emphasizes how happy she was with each of her husbands:

> Three husbands me, and I have
>   them enjoyed,
> Nor I by them, not they by me
>   annoyed.
> All lovely, loving all, some more,
>   some less;
> Though gone, their love and mem-
>   ory I bless. [118]

She expresses special fondness for her third husband and describes how he gave her unusual authority in their home and over their finances and household resources:

> Was never man so buxom [amiable]
>   to his wife;
> With him I led an easy darling's
>   life.
> I had my will in house, in purse, in
>   store;
> What would a woman old or
>   young have more? [119]

Writing Professionally

Women like Mary Herbert and Vittoria Colonna wrote for their personal satisfaction or to share their ideas with a circle of friends. These women did not challenge the Renaissance prohibition against women expressing themselves publicly. However, a few women—often because they needed to make a living for their families and saw writing as a way of doing this—were professional writers who had their work published.

Isabella Whitney is thought to be "the first declared professional woman poet in England." [120] Little is known about her life,

This sixteenth-century illustration depicts two female allegorical figures addressing letters to King Louis XII of France.

"No Man Bastard Be"

Catholics did not recognize Henry VIII's marriage to Anne Boleyn, Elizabeth's mother, and therefore saw Elizabeth as a bastard or illegitimate child. In addition, when Henry divorced Anne he declared Elizabeth illegitimate, although he later named Elizabeth in his will as his successor (after his son, Edward, and his elder daughter, Mary).

This background may be why Elizabeth chose to translate verses from the sixth-century Roman poet Boethius, who suggests that, because all people are children of God, they are all legitimate unless they commit bad deeds that separate them from their heavenly father (quoted in *The Poems of Queen Elizabeth I*):

What crake [boast] you of your stock
　[parentage]
　　Or forefathers old?
If your first spring and author
　God you view,

No man bastard be,
　Unless with vice the worst he feed
And leaveth so his birth.

Queen Elizabeth I was a brilliant poet and translator.

but she appears—unlike Mary Herbert or Vittoria Colonna—to have belonged to a lower-class family. One of her poems is addressed to her two younger sisters, who worked as servants in London, and it offers them advice on how to live and work respectably. It also gives a glimpse of the life of a Renaissance servant.

Your business [work] soon dispatch
　[complete]
　　And listen to no lies
Nor credit [believe] every fained
　[imaginary] tale
　　That many will devise [make up].
Your masters gone to bed
　Your mistresses at rest.

Their daughters all do haste above
   [upstairs]
   To get themselves undressed.
See that their plate [silverware] be
   safe
   And that no spoon do lack [is
   missing]
See doors and windows bolted fast
   [tight]
   For fear of any wrack [break-in].
Then help if need there be
   To do some household things.
If not—to bed, referring you,
   Unto the heavenly king.
Forgetting not to pray
   As I before you taught,
And giving thanks for all that he
Hath ever for you wrought
   [done]. [121]

A Heritage of Writing

Another woman who wrote profession-
ally was Lady Mary Wroth. She was the
niece of the writer Mary Herbert. Her
uncle, Sir Philip Sidney, had earned widespread fame for his poetry and prose, and
her father also wrote poems. She took
advantage of this writing background
when, at the age of twenty-seven, she was
widowed and needed to pay off her husband's debts. Wroth turned to writing as
a source of income. Her long book, called
The Countess of Montgomery's Arcadia, "con-
sists of a seemingly endless series of adven-
tures involving misplaced people, mistak-
en identities, trivial coincidences, lucky
meetings, and fortuitous endings to seemingly tragic sets of circumstances." [122] Yet
even this lighthearted story got her into
trouble. One nobleman, who believed he
had been satirized in the book, wrote that
she should "leave idle books alone, for wise
and worthier women have written none."
He angrily insisted that she should stick
to translation:

> Repent you of so many ill-spent years
> of so vain a book and . . . redeem the
> time [spent] with writing as large a
> volume of amorous toys [worthless
> love-stories] that at the last you may
> follow the rare and pious example of
> your virtuous and learned aunt, who
> translated so many godly books and
> especially the holy Psalms of David. [123]

"Spiritual Fun and Learning"

Few Renaissance women wrote plays or
acted, but in Italy there was a tradition of
nuns writing and performing plays. Their
plays carried valuable spiritual messages,
but they also provided entertainment for
the nuns and, in some cases, for visitors
and local townspeople too. One male play-
wright defended the nuns' right to stage
appropriate plays: "Everything . . . needs
to rest. For this reason, I believe, those who
established the convents saw fit to allow
the nuns to put on sacred plays and come-

dies in this season, making sure they were always above reproach [criticism] and apt to produce spiritual fun and learning." [124]

The nuns often performed their plays on feast days or other special occasions. Depending on the convent's resources, these could be quite elaborate productions, with scenery and costumes. Some men evidently objected, thinking it was unseemly for nuns to dress up, particularly as men. Playwrights outside the convent sometimes referred to this controversy. In one play, a male character says, "They dress like men with those tights and short pants and everything so that they look just like soldiers," and in another play a man objects, "Let them leave comedies . . . and stick to their spinning." [125]

One nun who wrote plays for her convent was Beatrice del Sera, who was born in 1515 and was placed in the convent when she was just two years old. She lived there all her life. Elissa Weaver, who has studied Beatrice's plays, explains how the nun's feelings about her life of confinement come out in one of her plays:

Female characters repeatedly protest being locked up. [One character in the play] says that if she were shut up

An Italian Renaissance theater troupe, including women members, is depicted in this sixteenth-century painting.

Renaissance women left behind a written record consisting of memoirs, translations, and poetry.

walled up she wouldn't call it Paradise. Another woman, imprisoned in the tower with [her friend] Aurabeatrice, tells her they were not born to be happy, but to be prisoners, slaves, subject to others. [126]

This play was not only a way for the nuns to alleviate their restricted lives with some "spiritual fun," but also an opportunity to voice frustration at being enclosed in the convent.

During the Renaissance all women, both secular and religious, were expected to remain silent, yet many women expressed themselves through their writing. Translators like Mary Herbert and Elizabeth I, through both their choice of texts to translate and the words they used, focused attention on what mattered to them. Memoirists like Charlotte Arbaleste recorded what they saw as significant, giving their own interpretation of events. And other women—from Italy to England, from the upper class to the lower orders—found their voice in poetry.

at home with only bread and water and her beloved husband, it would be Paradise, to which her sister responds that if she had ever experienced being

Chapter 8:
Women Artists

Art flourished during the Renaissance, and great art, including some of the greatest works in the Western world, was a hallmark of the era. Women joined men as patrons and appreciators of the Renaissance arts, but the reduction in women's rights and opportunities diminished their ability to train and work as artists. Both lower- and upper-class women were usually excluded from the profession, as Diane Moody explains:

The merging of arts and crafts with the subsequent control by the Guild system, coupled with a new emphasis in artistic training upon the study of the human body, made entry into this world hugely difficult for women: where once art had been made in convents or monasteries, it was now the product of a working-class artisan. . . . An influential framework was established for the education of upper-class girls where the skills of painting and drawing, along with musical talents, were regarded

as desirable and attractive attributes, to be mastered sufficiently to entertain and amuse a husband and his guests, but certainly not to be practiced outside the home.[127]

The women who succeeded in overcoming these obstacles have taken their place among the famous artists of the Renaissance. These outstanding individuals created remarkable paintings and sculptures that present a woman's perspective on life and ideas.

Working in Cherrystones and Marble

One of the first women artists known to have worked in Renaissance Italy was Properzia de Rossi, a sculptor from the city of Bologna. Her early work consisted of intricate carving on a minute scale that required extraordinary skill as well as patience. One example depicts the saints of the church—carved into a cherrystone. Sixty heads can be counted in this miniature piece. The fact that so tiny a work of art has survived into the twenty-first century demonstrates how highly it has been prized.

Later, Properzia created works in marble, and during the last decade of her life she won a number of public commissions. Historian Laura York describes the hostile environment in which Properzia made her name as a professional sculptor:

The men she competed with consistently maintained that women artists like Properzia were incapable of invention and of genius, and that public commissions (i.e., highly paid, visible works) should be reserved for those capable of ingenious creations (i.e., male artists). The increasing freedoms and individual fame male artists enjoyed did not extend to their female counterparts, who were judged as much, if not more, for their "deportment" and ladylike behavior as for their paintings, statues, and other works. [128]

"Making Them Appear Alive"

Sofonisba Anguissola was the daughter of an Italian nobleman who apparently did value artistic talent in girls, for in 1546 he sent both Sofonisba and her younger sister, Elena, to study painting with a well-known master, Bernardino Campi. Their training was not the same as that given to boys, however, for girls were not allowed to be apprentices in the artist's workshop. Instead, Sofonisba and Elena lived and worked as paying guests in Campi's home, where they learned artistic techniques by copying some of his paintings. Sofonisba later taught these techniques to her younger sisters, Lucia, Anna Maria, and Europa.

Because she was not permitted to draw the naked male form—a subject that was important in depicting scenes from the Bible and classical mythology—Anguissola had to focus on other themes. She completed a large number of self-portraits, and one of her best-known paintings, *The Chess Game,* shows her sisters Lucia, Minerva, and Europa dressed in fine clothes and jewelry and playing chess on a small table that is covered by an oriental carpet. The artist and writer Giorgio Vasari, having heard of Anguissola and her talented sisters, went to see for himself and wrote, "I have this year seen a picture in her father's house at Cremona, most carefully finished, representing her three sisters playing at chess, in the company of an old lady of the house, making them appear alive and lacking speech only." [129] This painting is remarkable, not only for the liveliness that struck Vasari, but also because paintings of this nature—known as "conversation pieces"—were rarely produced at that time. They did not become common until the following century.

Anguissola achieved fame as a portrait painter, and she was invited to the Span-

Sofonisba Anguissola trained with a professional painter. She appears here in one of her many self-portraits.

ish court, where she lived as a painter and an art teacher. When Pope Pius IV received a portrait of the Spanish queen that he had commissioned, he wrote to thank Anguissola, saying, "We thank you and assure you that we shall treasure it among our choicest possessions, and commend your marvelous talent which is the least among your numerous virtues."[130] Anguissola lived into her nineties, and

A Painterly Joke

Sofonisba Anguissola was unusual among women artists of the Renaissance, having received professional training by the artist Bernardino Campi. One of her best-known works is a painting of Campi. It amounts to a double portrait because it shows him working on a portrait of Anguissola herself. But there is a difference in the quality of the two faces in the portrait that could be seen as a criticism of the tutor's skill. In *The Obstacle Race*, Germaine Greer suggests that the painting "seems to be Sofonisba's painterly joke. The head of Campi is subtly expressive, in her own best manner, while her version of his version of herself is blank and moon-faced, larger than life."

though her vision failed and she could no longer paint, she was given a pension by the Spanish court. However, the officials who were to pay her did not believe that a woman could live to such a great age. They required her to prove that she was still alive before they would dispense the money.

Earning Fame "Outside the Feminine Sphere"

Anguissola provided advice and encouragement to many young artists who were striving to win commissions. One of these was Lavinia Fontana. As the daughter of a painter, Fontana grew up in an artistic environment and, although she was not permitted to enter her father's workshop as a student, learned the skills of painting at home. When she was twenty-five and involved in marriage negotiations, a friend named Orazio Sammachini wrote of her,

"If she lives a few years she will be able to draw great profit from her painting, as well as being god-fearing and of purest life and handsome manners."[131] As Sammachini predicted, Fontana achieved fame and won numerous well-paid commissions. In addition, she fulfilled the role of wife and mother.

During the marriage negotiations, Fontana painted a portrait of herself as a gift to her fiancé's family. This self-portrait shows her playing a clavichord (a keyboard instrument) while a servant holds a music book in the background. This painting—which resembles a self-portrait by Anguissola, whom Fontana knew and admired—gave her fiancé's father his first glimpse of the bride. In his opinion she appeared "not fair and not ugly, but just in the middle, as women have to be."[132]

Fontana earned a reputation for portraiture and also won a number of significant commissions for religious works to be hung in churches. Portrait painting was a sphere where women artists could often find work because wealthy men preferred that their wives and daughters pose for a female rather than a male artist for the many hours necessary to complete a painting. Religious work, however, was hard for a woman artist to secure. Many religious paintings were frescoes, which had to be painted directly onto walls. It was thought improper for women to paint in public places, so fresco commissions were usually given to men, yet Fontana's success meant that she received commissions for large-scale works in public buildings. She overcame the restrictions by painting large canvasses in her studio. In addition, Fontana was well paid, earning one thousand ducats for a commission by the king of Spain, while a famous male artist, Annibale Carracci, made only eight hundred ducats for

Anguissola's painting of her sisters playing chess was highly praised by Renaissance artist Giorgio Vasari.

a similar painting. When Fontana died her sons described her as a painter "whose fame reached outside the feminine sphere."[133]

"One Could Not Desire Anything More"

Another artist who may have been influenced by Sofonisba Anguissola was Fede Galizia, whose naturalistic style of portraiture resembles hers. As a teenager, Galizia was already well known for her portraiture. Her skill was especially admired by

Portraits like this one of an Italian gentleman earned Fede Galizia fame even as a teenager.

the historian and scholar Paolo Morigia, who became one of her patrons. Describing a portrait she painted of him, he wrote that the work was "of such excellence, and such a good likeness, that one could not desire anything more."[134]

Although she initially gained fame for her portrait painting, Galizia's still-life paintings are considered among her greatest works. She produced warmly lit paintings of peaches and pears lying in metal dishes and woven baskets, and her ability is evident in the varying textures she represented. By the time of her death, probably from the plague, in 1630 Galizia had earned an international reputation for both her portraits and her still-life paintings.

"If I Were a Man . . ."

Like many early modern women artists, Artemisia Gentileschi was the daughter of a painter and practiced her art at home. Yet her education as an artist led her into great peril when Agostino Tassi, a colleague of her father who was expected to tutor her, raped her instead. He initially promised to marry her, but then denied the whole affair and accused her of promiscuity. Since women had no rights under the laws of the time, it was Gentileschi's father who sued Tassi, on the basis that the rape resulted in damaged property: a daughter who was now unmarriageable. Over the course of a seven-month trial Gentileschi spoke out fear-

Artemisia Gentileschi produced five paintings, including this one, of the heroine Judith beheading Holofernes.

lessly against her attacker, even when she was tortured.

During the trial, Gentileschi had to undergo physical examinations to determine the date of her loss of virginity. She was also subjected to the *sibille* (thumbscrew)—a type of torturous early lie detector consisting of cords wrapped around the fingers and tightened. During the questioning, while Tassi looked on, she reiterated her innocence, shouting at her violator, "This is the ring you give me, and these are your promises!"[135]

The courage that Gentileschi showed in this ordeal stayed with her and became the basis of her highly successful career in painting. She is famous for her powerful depictions of women in mythology and the Bible, many of them showing scenes of great violence. She produced five paintings of the legendary heroine Judith, who saved the Hebrews by beheading the Assyrian general Holofernes. Theodore K. Rabb describes one of these:

> What is arguably her most powerful painting, alive with so much immediacy, drama, violence, and slashing contrasts of light and dark . . . is a *Judith Slaying Holofernes* that rivets the attention to the half-severed head and the blood gushing from the wound. This was a sufficiently famous image to inspire engraved copies for wider distribution. Nor is the theme of a woman's struggles (and rare triumphs) in a man's world hard to find in the other stories she depicted. [136]

Gentileschi's talent caught the attention of influential patrons, including Michelangelo's great-nephew and King Charles I of England, who was one of the great collectors of the time. She was the first woman to be admitted into the city of Florence's acclaimed artistic academy, the Accademia del Disegno, where her friend Galileo was also a member.

Yet even a woman artist of Gentileschi's high reputation had to struggle to be treated fairly in an overwhelmingly male environment. Her letters reveal how forcefully she insisted on fair payment for her work. To one patron she wrote, "I was mortified to hear that you wanted to deduct one third from the already low price I had asked. I must tell Your Lordship that this is impossible, and that I cannot accept a reduction, both because of the value of the painting and my great need." In another letter she refuses to send a preliminary drawing:

> I have made a solemn vow never to send my drawings because people have cheated me. Just today I found that, having done a drawing of souls in Purgatory for the Bishop, he, in order to spend less, commissioned another painter to do the painting using my work. If I were a man, I can't imagine it would have turned out this way. [137]

Artemisia Gentileschi is now acknowledged as one of the foremost artists of the period. Yet after her death she was forgotten—except as the allegedly promiscuous woman at the center of a rape trial—and her father was given credit for many of her paintings. Only recently have art historians restored Gentileschi to her proper place as one of the greatest painters of her time.

A Growing Market for Art in Northern Europe

While the Italian nobility fostered art and the church encouraged religious architecture and painting there, northern Europe also experienced an upsurge in art

Boiling Dried Rabbit Skins

Renaissance artists had to prepare their own materials, and the quality of their art depended in part on the quality of the surface they were painting on and of the paints themselves. Writing in *Women in World History: A Biographical Encyclopedia,* edited by Anne Commine, Diane Moody explains that

artists of the time had to be able to mix natural pigments to make their own oil paints, having first prepared an oil base by a laborious cooking process. The canvas or panel that was to be painted upon also demanded tedious preparation, involving the boiling of dried rabbit skins to make a type of glue that was applied in thin layers before painting took place.

When a boy joined an artist's workshop, he would be put to work at these tasks and would get to know the best techniques and materials to use in each painting. Girls, because they rarely had access to a painter's workshop, usually could learn these important skills only at home, from a family member who was an artist.

in the sixteenth and seventeenth centuries. As Moody points out:

A growing middle class, made rich by the fruits of trade, eagerly adorned its pristine homes with material displays of wealth and taste. In this Protestant nation, the bourgeoisie, not the church, became the prime patrons of one of the most popular art markets ever seen, keeping prices affordable and encouraging artists to specialize to ensure a place within it. [138]

A few notable women were able to overcome the barriers to their work as artists and participate in this dynamic market for art.

Levina Teerlinc was an artist from Flanders (in today's Belgium), who specialized in painting miniature portraits. These tiny, detailed portraits were not designed to be displayed on a wall. Instead they were carried or incorporated into a piece of jewelry. Around 1546 Teerlinc moved to England, where she earned a salary as an artist to Henry VIII and his court. She remained in England after Henry's death and worked for three more Tudor monarchs: Edward VI, Mary Tudor, and Elizabeth I.

Teerlinc's work was highly valued by the Tudor kings and queens, who were acutely aware of how their appearance—and the way they were shown in portraits—contributed to the impression of majesty

Flemish artist Clara Peeters painted this still life and is credited with being one of the originators of the genre.

they needed to present to maintain their hold on power. Art historian Germaine Greer explains that they particularly valued the miniature portraits that were Teerlinc's specialty:

> The greatest artists of their time worked willingly in the tiniest scale, and there is some evidence that their smaller works were more highly prized. Levina Teerlinc was handsomely rewarded

by the monarchs for her miniatures, for which she earned forty pounds a year, more than [the artist Hans] Holbein, who also worked in larger format. [139]

Pioneering the Genre of Still-Life Painting

Still-life paintings, depicting household objects became popular in northern Europe in the 1600s. Art historians have traced this trend to a woman artist named Clara Peeters, who worked in Antwerp, a Belgian city that was an important center for art. Little is known about Peeters's life, but she completed her earliest known painting in 1608 when she was fourteen or fifteen years old. It is one of the first examples of Flemish still-life painting. According to art historians Ann Sutherland Harris and Linda Nochlin, "fewer than ten paintings of flowers and fewer than five of food" predate Peeters's 1608 painting, and "thus she would appear to be one of the originators of the genre." [140]

Peeters's paintings demonstrate her skill at representing a range of different shapes and textures: the soft petals of flowers, the shiny surface of a china bowl, the shadows of a golden chain, the curves of shells. In addition, she sometimes included tiny portraits of herself reflected in the objects she depicted. Greer has described one of Peeters's paintings, a still life dating from 1612:

It shows three tall vessels, a pottery vase of anemones, hyacinths, tulips and a snakeshead lily, and two gilt cups with covers standing about a Chinese celadon [green glazed] bowl out of which hangs a golden chain.... On the shiny bosses [knobs] of the furthermost cup, Clara Peeters has carefully painted her own reflection in miniature, six times, in the flare of light from a window. [141]

By including these tiny self-portraits, Peeters showed her skill in portraiture as well as still life. The reflections of her face also bring Peeters's identity into her work, and today's art historians—who often have trouble determining who created a piece of art—use these clues in attributing Renaissance paintings.

Painting from a Woman's Point of View

The problems of establishing an artist's identity have been specially troublesome in the case of the Dutch painter Judith Leyster, "who, though highly respected in her own lifetime, suffered from misattribution to the extent that she became only a footnote in writings on the works of her husband or tutor." [142] Now, however, she is again highly respected and seen as one of the foremost artists of Holland's golden age of art.

Leyster studied with the famous artist Frans Hals, and in 1633 she was admitted into the Guild of St. Luke, the first woman to be accorded this professional honor. As a member of the guild, Leyster was able to set up her own workshop, where she tutored students and developed the style for which she gained fame. According to writer Ruth Ashby:

Leyster especially excelled at genre paintings—scenes of people in everyday situations. Her paintings are

Women Musicians

Many Renaissance paintings—including self-portraits by Anguissola and Fontana and a painting of musicians by Leyster—show women in the role of musicians, yet few Renaissance women have been identified as performers or composers. Many professional musicians at the time worked for the Catholic Church, but church positions were not open to women.

Tarquinia Molza is one woman who is known to have been a successful musician. She was a singer and may also have played the viol (a stringed instrument played with a bow) and composed songs. Her friend Francesco Patrizi, a writer and philosopher, wrote about Molza in his work *L'Amorosa Filosofia*. He describes her performance at a banquet for Alfonso d'Este II, Duke of Ferrara, who was visiting Modena on a state visit. The duke was so captivated by her song that he asked her to repeat it several times and then invited her to sit at his table. Some years later she accepted a position at the duke's court in Ferrara, where she directed a group of female singers called the Concerto Delle Donne. These women are considered the first professional women musicians, but because female musicians were unknown at the time, they were officially hired as ladies-in-waiting to the duke's wife.

Women musicians were often the subject of Renaissance paintings, yet few women have been identified as performers or composers.

dramatically lit, often by only one candle. She picked popular subjects: people having a good time, drinking, dancing, playing the fiddle or the flute. Sometimes she portrayed women at home doing domestic chores, sewing, or caring for children. One of her most famous works, *The Proposition* (1631), shows a woman rejecting a man's advances. The young woman, bent over her sewing, completely ignores an older man who holds out a handful of coins to her, presumably the payment he would give her for sexual favors. Her calm self-sufficiency clearly marks this as a subject painted from a woman's point of view. [143]

After Leyster's marriage in 1636 to another painter, her output decreased because her time was taken up with child-birth, her children's illnesses, and her husband's legal disputes. However, in 1643 she benefited from "tulipomania," the fashion for rare flower bulbs that swept Holland. Bulb merchants needed lavishly illustrated catalogues to support their sales, and Leyster contracted to provide paintings for this purpose. "For Leyster," Moody explains, "this meant small-scale work that could more easily be combined with the role of mother and housewife, while also providing a source of family income." [144]

Some Renaissance women artists, like Lavinia Fontana and Artemisia Gentileschi, won fame in their own time. Others, like Levina Teerlinc, Clara Peeters, and Judith Leyster, achieved great commercial success. All left artworks that give today's viewers the opportunity to perceive the world through the eyes of a gifted, highly skilled woman at the dawn of the early modern era.

Notes

Chapter 1: Wives, Mothers, and Caregivers

1. Quoted in Margaret J.M. Ezell, *The Patriarch's Wife: Literary Evidence and the History of the Family.* Chapel Hill: University of North Carolina Press, 1987, p. 38.
2. Sara Mendelson and Patricia Crawford, *Women in Early Modern England, 1550–1720.* Oxford: Oxford University Press, 1998, p. 38.
3. Joy Wiltenburg, *Disorderly Women and Female Power in the Street Literature of Early Modern England and Germany.* Charlottesville: University Press of Virginia, 1992, p. 76.
4. Quoted in Ezell, *Patriarch's Wife,* p. 33.
5. Quoted in Stanley Chojnacki, "'The Most Serious Duty': Motherhood, Gender, and Patrician Culture in Renaissance Venice," in Marilyn Migiel and Juliana Schiesari, eds., *Refiguring Women: Perspectives on Gender and the Italian Renaissance.* Ithaca, NY: Cornell University Press, 1991, p. 133.
6. Mendelson and Crawford, *Women in Early Modern England,* p. 38.
7. Quoted in Alan Macfarlane, *Marriage and Love in England: Modes of Reproduction, 1300–1840.* Oxford: Basil Blackwell, 1986, p. 202.
8. Quoted in Macfarlane, *Marriage and Love in England,* p. 203.
9. Mendelson and Crawford, *Women in Early Modern England,* p. 140.
10. Mendelson and Crawford, *Women in Early Modern England,* pp. 140–41.
11. Katherine Duncan-Jones, *Sir Philip Sidney: Courtier Poet.* New Haven, CT: Yale University Press, 1991, p. 8.
12. Merry E. Wiesner, *Women and Gender in Early Modern Europe,* 2nd ed. Cambridge: Cambridge University Press, 2000, p. 115.
13. Merry E. Wiesner, "Early Modern Midwifery: A Case Study," *International Journal of Women's Studies,* January/February 1983, p. 26.
14. Wiesner, "Early Modern Midwifery," p. 27.
15. Wiesner, *Women and Gender,* pp. 115–16.
16. Quoted in Diane Willen, "Women in the Public Sphere in Early Modern England: The Case of the Urban Working Poor," *Sixteenth Century Journal,* 1988, p. 563.

17. Thomas G. Benedek, "The Changing Relationship Between Midwives and Physicians During the Renaissance," *Bulletin of the History of Medicine*, 1977, p. 563.

18. Benedek, "The Changing Relationship," p. 563.

19. Quoted in Mendelson and Crawford, *Women in Early Modern England,* p. 118.

20. Quoted in Merry E. Wiesner, *Working Women in Renaissance Germany.* New Brunswick, NJ: Rutgers University Press, 1986, p. 52.

21. Quoted in Benedek, "The Changing Relationship," p. 563.

22. Quoted in Wiesner, *Working Women,* p. 52.

Chapter 2: Women at Work

23. Wiesner, *Women and Gender,* p. 107.

24. Mendelson and Crawford, *Women in Early Modern England,* p. 274.

25. Barbara Hanawalt, ed., *Women and Work in Preindustrial Europe.* Bloomington: Indiana University Press, 1986, p. xvi.

26. Mendelson and Crawford, *Women in Early Modern England,* pp. 270–71.

27. Wiesner, *Women and Gender,* p. 111.

28. Christiane Klapisch-Zuber, "Women Servants in Florence During the Fourteenth and Fifteenth Centuries," in Hanawalt, *Women and Work in Preindustrial Europe,* pp. 72–73.

29. Quoted in Wiesner, *Women and Gender,* p. 119.

30. J. C. Appleby, "Women and Piracy in Ireland: From Grainne O'Malley to Anne Bonney," in Margaret MacCurtain and Mary O'Dowd, eds., *Women in Early Modern Ireland, 1500–1800.* Edinburgh: Edinburgh University Press, 1991, p. 62.

31. Quoted in Wiesner, *Women and Gender,* p. 109.

32. Mendelson and Crawford, *Women in Early Modern England,* p. 278.

33. Mendelson and Crawford, *Women in Early Modern England,* p. 276.

34. Mendelson and Crawford, *Women in Early Modern England,* p. 265.

35. Judith M. Bennett, *Ale, Beer and Brewsters in England: Women's Work in a Changing World, 1300–1600.* New York: Oxford University Press, 1996, p. 55.

36. Bennett, *Ale, Beer and Brewsters,* p. 91.

37. Bennett, *Ale, Beer and Brewsters,* p. 91.

38. Wiltenburg, *Disorderly Women and Female Power,* p. 10.

39. Quoted in Natalie Zemon Davis, "Women in the Crafts in Sixteenth-Century Lyon," in Hanawalt, *Women and Work in Preindustrial Europe,* p. 167.

40. Quoted in Davis, "Women in the Crafts," p. 167.

41. Quoted in Davis, "Women in the Crafts," p. 176.

42. Wiesner, *Working Women,* p. 168.

Chapter 3: Women in Religious Life

43. Wiesner, *Women and Gender,* p. 222.
44. Wiesner, *Women and Gender,* p. 222.
45. Chojnacki, "'The Most Serious Duty,'" p. 144.
46. Margaret L. King, *Women of the Renaissance.* Chicago: University of Chicago Press, 1991, p. 83.
47. Quoted in King, *Women of the Renaissance,* p. 97.
48. Quoted in Theodore K. Rabb, *Renaissance Lives: Portraits of an Age.* New York: Pantheon, 1993, p. 97.
49. Quoted in Rabb, *Renaissance Lives,* p. 108.
50. Quoted in Alison Weber, *Teresa of Avila and the Rhetoric of Femininity.* Princeton, NJ: Princeton University Press, 1990, pp. 3–4.
51. Wiesner, *Women and Gender,* p. 229.
52. Wiesner, *Women and Gender,* p. 231.
53. Mendelson and Crawford, *Women in Early Modern England,* pp. 310–11.
54. Mendelson and Crawford, *Women in Early Modern England,* p. 311.
55. Mendelson and Crawford, *Women in Early Modern England,* p. 311.
56. Quoted in Wiesner, *Women and Gender,* p. 222.
57. Quoted in Wiesner, *Women and Gender,* p. 223.
58. Quoted in Wiesner, *Women and Gender,* p. 223.
59. Quoted in Wiesner, *Women and Gender,* p. 223.
60. King, *Women of the Renaissance,* p. 137.
61. Quoted in King, *Women of the Renaissance,* p. 137.
62. Quoted in Anne Commine, ed., *Women in World History: A Biographical Encyclopedia,* Detroit: Yorkin, 1999.
63. Wiesner, *Working Women,* pp. 46–47.

Chapter 4: Renaissance Queens

64. Quoted in Hester W. Chapman, *Lady Jane Grey: October 1537–February 1554.* London: Pan, 1962, p. 94.
65. Quoted in Commine, *Women in World History.*
66. Quoted in Commine, *Women in World History.*
67. Quoted in Irene Mahoney, *Madame Catherine.* New York: Coward, McCann & Geoghegan, 1975, p. 30.
68. Quoted in Mahoney, *Madame Catherine,* p. 39.
69. Quoted in Rabb, *Renaissance Lives,* p. 135.
70. Quoted in Mahoney, *Madame Catherine,* p. 106.
71. Quoted in Mahoney, *Madame Catherine,* p. 106.
72. Pearl Hogrefe, *Women of Action in Tudor England: Nine Biographical Sketches.* Ames: Iowa State University Press, 1977, p. 232.

73. Hogrefe, *Women of Action,* p. 217.

74. Quoted in Alison Weir, *The Life of Elizabeth I.* New York: Ballantine, 1998, p. 393.

75. Quoted in Weir, *The Life of Queen Elizabeth I,* p. 487.

76. Quoted in Commine, *Women in World History.*

77. Quoted in Commine, *Women in World History.*

Chapter 5: Women Rebels: Politicians to Pirates

78. Quoted in Commine, *Women in World History.*

79. Quoted in Commine, *Women in World History.*

80. Mendelson and Crawford, *Women in Early Modern England,* pp. 337–38.

81. Quoted in Duncan-Jones, *Sir Philip Sidney,* p. 4.

82. Duncan-Jones, *Sir Philip Sidney,* pp. 6–7.

83. Quoted in Commine, *Women in World History.*

84. Quoted in Ernst Breisach, *Caterina Sforza: A Renaissance Virago.* Chicago: University of Chicago Press, 1967, p. 239.

85. Quoted in Anny Latour, *The Borgias.* London: Elek, 1963, p. 140.

86. Wiesner, *Working Women,* p. 125.

87. Barrett Beer, *Rebellion and Riot: Popular Disorder in England During the Reign of Edward VI.* Kent, OH: Kent State University Press, 1982, p. 56.

88. Quoted in Wiltenburg, *Disorderly Women and Female Power,* p. 191.

89. Quoted in Wiltenburg, *Disorderly Women and Female Power,* p. 192.

90. Ulrike Klausmann, Marion Meinzerin, and Gabriel Kuhn, *Women Pirates and the Politics of the Jolly Roger,* trans. Tyler Austin and Nicholas Levis. Montreal: Black Rose, 1997, p. 150.

91. Anne Chambers, "'The Pirate Queen of Ireland': Grace O'Malley," in Jo Stanley, ed., *Bold in Her Breeches: Women Pirates Across the Ages.* San Francisco: Pandora, 1995, p. 101.

92. Quoted in Chambers, "'The Pirate Queen of Ireland,'" p. 95.

93. Quoted in Chambers, "'The Pirate Queen of Ireland,'" p. 96.

Chapter 6: Women Scholars and Scientists

94. Jacqueline Eales, *Women in Early Modern England, 1500–1700.* London: UCL, Taylor & Francis, 1998, p. 13.

95. King, *Women of the Renaissance,* p. 164.

96. Quoted in King, *Women of the Renaissance,* p. 194.

97. King, *Women of the Renaissance,* pp. 139–40.

98. King, *Women of the Renaissance,* p. 178.

99. Quoted in King, *Women of the Renaissance,* p. 196.

100. Margaret Leah King, "Thwarted Ambitions: Six Learned Women of the Italian Renaissance," *Soundings,* 1976, p. 285.

101. King, *Women of the Renaissance,* p. 199.

102. Roy T. Matthews and F. DeWitt Platt, *The Western Humanities.* Mountain View, CA: Mayfield, 1998, p. 279.

103. C.J. Blaisdell, "Marguerite de Navarre and Her Circle," in J.R. Brink, ed., *Female Scholars: A Tradition of Learned Women Before 1800.* Montreal: Eden, 1980, p. 37.

104. C.F. Black et al., *Cultural Atlas of the Renaissance.* New York: Prentice-Hall, 1993, p. 104.

105. Quoted in Lynette Hunter and Sarah Hutton, eds., *Women, Science and Medicine, 1500–1700: Mothers and Sisters of the Royal Society.* Gloucestershire, UK: Sutton, 1997, p. 3.

106. Lynette Hunter, "Women and Domestic Medicine: Lady Experimenters, 1570–1620," in Hunter and Hutton, *Women, Science and Medicine,* p. 96.

107. *The Biographical Dictionary of Women in Science.*

108. Maria Vintro and Mary Ellen Waithe, "Doña Oliva Sabuco," www.sabuco.org.

109. Vintro and Waithe, "Doña Oliva Sabuco."

Chapter 7: Women Writers

110. Margaret P. Hannay, *Philip's Phoenix: Mary Sidney, Countess of Pembroke.* Oxford: Oxford University Press, 1990, p. 62.

111. Hannay, *Philip's Phoenix,* p. 129.

112. Quoted in Weir, *The Life of Elizabeth I,* p. 416.

113. Betty Travitsky, ed., *The Paradise of Women: Writings by Englishwomen of the Renaissance.* Westport, CT: Greenwood, 1981, p. 37.

114. Natalie Zemon Davis, "Gender and Genre: Women as Historical Writers, 1400–1820," in Patricia H. Labalme, ed., *Beyond Their Sex: Learned Women of the European Past.* New York: New York University Press, 1980, p. 162.

115. Charlotte Arbaleste de Mornay, *A Huguenot Family in the XVI Century: The Memoirs of Philippe de Mornay, Sieur du Plessis Marly, Written by His Wife,* trans. Lucy Crump. New York: E.P. Dutton, 1926, p. 120.

116. Katharina M. Wilson, ed., *Women Writers of the Renaissance and Reformation.* Athens: University of Georgia Press, 1987, p. 35.

117. Robert C. Evans and Anne C. Little, eds., *"The Muses Females Are": Martha Moulsworth and Other Women Writers of the English Renaissance.* West Cornwall, CT: Locust Hill, 1995, p. 217.

118. Evans and Little, *"The Muses Females Are,"* p. 217.

119. Evans and Little, *"The Muses Females Are,"* p. 218.

120. Travitsky, *Paradise of Women,* p. 117.

121. Travitsky, *Paradise of Women,* pp. 118–19.

122. Travitsky, *Paradise of Women,* p. 135.

123. Quoted in Gary Waller, *English Poetry of the Sixteenth Century.* New York: Longman, 1986, p. 267.

124. Quoted in Elissa Weaver, "Spiritual Fun: A Study of Sixteenth-Century Tuscan Convent Theater," in Mary Beth Rose, ed., *Women in the Middle Ages and the Renaissance: Literary and Historical Perspectives.* Syracuse, NY: New York University Press, 1986, p. 176.

125. Quoted in Weaver, "Spiritual Fun," p. 182.

126. Weaver, "Spiritual Fun," p. 176.

Chapter 8: Women Artists

127. Quoted in Commine, *Women in World History.*

128. Quoted in Commine, *Women in World History.*

129. Quoted in ommine, *Women in World History.*

130. Quoted in Commine, *Women in World History.*

131. Quoted in Germaine Greer, *The Obstacle Race.* New York: Farrar Straus Giroux, 1979, p. 210.

132. Quoted in Commine, *Women in World History.*

133. Quoted in Commine, *Women in World History.*

134. Quoted in Commine, *Women in World History.*

135. Quoted in Commine, *Women in World History.*

136. Rabb, *Renaissance Lives,* p. 185.

137. Quoted in Rabb, *Renaissance Lives,* pp. 188, 190.

138. Quoted in Commine, *Women in World History.*

139. Greer, *Obstacle Race,* p. 113.

140. Ann Sutherland Harris and Linda Nochlin, *Women Artists, 1550–1950.* Los Angeles: Los Angeles County Museum of Art, 1976, p. 128.

141. Greer, *Obstacle Race,* p. 235.

142. Quoted in Commine, *Women in World History.*

143. Ruth Ashby and Deborah Gore Ohrn, eds., *Herstory.* New York: Viking, 1995, p. 5.

144. Quoted in Commine, *Women in World History.*

For Further Reading

Books

Ruth Ashby and Deborah Gore Ohrn, eds., *Herstory.* New York: Viking, 1995. Short biographies of influential women throughout history. Includes a vivid portrait of Artemisia Gentileschi.

Ruth Dean and Melissa Thomson, *Women of the Middle Ages.* San Diego: Lucent, 2003. Describes the many different roles filled by European women in the centuries that preceded the Renaissance.

William W. Lace, *Elizabeth I and Her Court.* San Diego: Lucent, 2002. Portrays the life of England's great Renaissance queen and the courtiers who served her.

Milton Meltzer, *Ten Queens: Portraits of Women in Power.* New York: Dutton, 1998. This illustrated volume covers a two-thousand-year time span. Includes chapters on Isabella of Castile and Elizabeth I.

Don Nardo, *Women Leaders of Nations.* San Diego: Lucent, 1999. An overview of powerful women in history from ancient times to the twentieth century. Includes chapters on Queen Isabella of Castile and Queen Elizabeth I of England.

Patricia D. Netzley, *Life During the Renaissance.* San Diego: Lucent, 1997. Describes the history, culture, and everyday life of the Renaissance.

Theodore K. Rabb, *Renaissance Lives: Portraits of an Age.* New York: Pantheon, 1993. Presents brief but vivid portraits of many of the era's well-known personalities.

Gail B. Stewart, *Life in Elizabethan London.* San Diego: Lucent, 2002. Describes what it would be like for an outsider visiting Elizabethan London for the first time.

Clarice Swisher, *Elizabethan England: Primary Sources.* San Diego: Lucent, 2002. Documents concerning life in England under Elizabeth I.

Web Sites

Doña Oliva Sabuco (www.sabuco.org). Information about the life and times of a remarkable Spanish woman scientist.

4000 Years of Women in Science (www.astr.ua.edu/4000WS/4000WS.html). Records the contributions of women to science throughout history.

Granuaile O'Malley Web Resources (www.omalleyclan.org/uow/omalley_web/granuaile.htm). Part of the O'Malley Clan Association Web site.

Offers links to information on Grace O'Malley; a list of recommended books and music; and photos of castles and other places relevant to the pirate queen's life.

Renaissance: What Inspired This Age of Balance and Order? (www.learner.org/exhibits/renaissance). Information on many aspects of the Renaissance, with a focus on Italy. Includes links to primary source documents.

Sound Recordings

Full Well She Sang: Women's Music from the Middle Ages and Renaissance. Performed by Toronto Consort. SRI Canada. Includes madrigals by Renaissance women.

The Secret Music of Luzzascho Luzzaschi: Madrigals for the Ladies of Ferrara. Performed by Musica Secreta. Amon Ra, 1996. Songs that were performed by Tarquinia Molza and her group of singers.

Songs of Ecstasy and Devotion from a 17th Century Italian Convent. Performed by Musica Secreta. Linn Records, 1999. Religious music from a late Renaissance convent.

Works Consulted

Books

Jack Anderson, *Ballet and Modern Dance: A Concise History*. Princeton, NJ: Princeton, 1986. This history of dance begins with an account of how Catherine de Médicis staged the first ballet.

Charlotte Arbaleste de Mornay, *A Huguenot Family in the XVI Century: The Memoirs of Philippe de Mornay, Sieur du Plessis Marly, Written by His Wife*. Trans. Lucy Crump. New York: E.P. Dutton, 1926. A French Protestant woman's account of her life and her husband's, written for their son.

Barrett Beer, *Rebellion and Riot: Popular Disorder in England During the Reign of Edward VI*. Kent, OH: Kent State University Press, 1982. A detailed discussion of unrest under the Tudor kings of England, with only glancing references to the participation of women.

Elaine V. Beilin, *Redeeming Eve: Women Writers of the English Renaissance*. Princeton, NJ: Princeton University Press, 1987. Discusses the works of the leading women writers of the English Renaissance.

Judith M. Bennett, *Ale, Beer and Brewsters in England: Women's Work in a Changing World, 1300–1600*. New York: Oxford University Press, 1996. Discusses the challenges women faced in business during the Renaissance, tracing the decline of brewing beer, a traditional income source for women.

Olivier Bernier, *The Renaissance Princes*. Chicago: Stonehenge, 1983. Accounts of the lives of Italian leaders. Illustrated in color. Includes a chapter on Isabella d'Este.

C.F. Black et al., *Cultural Atlas of the Renaissance*. New York: Prentice-Hall, 1993. An illustrated overview volume discussing many different elements of Renaissance culture.

Ernst Breisach, *Caterina Sforza: A Renaissance Virago*. Chicago: University of Chicago Press, 1967. The life and times of a remarkable woman who belonged to a powerful Italian family.

Renate Bridenthal, Claudia Koonz, and Susan Stuard, eds., *Becoming Visible: Women in European History*. Boston: Houghton Mifflin, 1987. Academic articles on Renaissance issues, including Joan Kelly's "Did Women Have a Renaissance?"

J.R. Brink, ed., *Female Scholars: A Tradition of Learned Women Before 1800*. Montreal: Eden, 1980. A collection of articles that includes some on the very few Renaissance women who became known for their learning.

Anne Chambers, *Granuaile: The Life and Times of Grace O'Malley, 1530–1603.* Dublin: Wolfhound, 1988. A well-researched biography of the legendary Irish pirate queen.

Hester W. Chapman, *Lady Jane Grey: October 1537–February 1554.* London: Pan, 1962. For the general reader, a biography of Lady Jane Grey, who was queen of England for nine days.

Anne Commine, ed., *Women in World History: A Biographical Encyclopedia.* Detroit: Yorkin, 1999. Short biographies of influential women from all walks of life, including the outstanding women of the Renaissance. Provides some bibliographical information.

Katherine Duncan-Jones, *Sir Philip Sidney: Courtier Poet.* New Haven, CT: Yale University Press, 1991. This biography focuses on the relationship between events in the poet's life and his poetry.

Jacqueline Eales, *Women in Early Modern England, 1500–1700.* London: UCL, Taylor & Francis, 1998. Discusses women's roles and experiences but focuses on governmental actions rather than on individuals.

Elizabeth I, *The Poems of Queen Elizabeth I.* Providence, RI: Brown University Press, 1964. Original poems and translations by England's Renaissance queen. Includes explanatory notes.

Robert C. Evans and Anne C. Little, eds., *"The Muses Female Are": Martha Moulsworth and Other Women Writers of the English Renaissance.* West Cornwall, CT: Locust Hill, 1995.

Margaret J.M. Ezell, *The Patriarch's Wife: Literary Evidence and the History of the Family.* Chapel Hill: University of North Carolina Press, 1987. Discusses the many ways in which Renaissance culture molded women's lives from childhood through marriage and into widowhood.

Moira Ferguson, ed., *First Feminists: British Women Writers, 1578–1799.* Bloomington: Indiana University Press, 1985. Presents the writing of many Englishwomen, with explanatory introductions.

Germaine Greer, *The Obstacle Race.* New York: Farrar Straus Giroux, 1979. An illustrated survey of women artists through the ages with commentary on specific works of art. Focuses on the centuries-old neglect of women's art.

Barbara Hanawalt, ed., *Women and Work in Preindustrial Europe.* Bloomington: Indiana University Press, 1986. Essays on medieval and Renaissance women's work in a variety of European cultures.

Margaret P. Hannay, *Philip's Phoenix: Mary Sidney, Countess of Pembroke.*

Oxford: Oxford University Press, 1990. An account of the life and writing of Mary Sidney Herbert, sister of the famous poet and diplomat Sir Philip Sidney.

Ann Sutherland Harris and Linda Nochlin, *Women Artists, 1550–1950.* Los Angeles: Los Angeles County Museum of Art, 1976. An illustrated exhibition catalog that discusses the lives and works of women artists over four centuries.

Katherine Usher Henderson and Barbara F. McManus, eds., *Half Humankind: Contexts and Texts of the Controversy About Women in England, 1540–1640.* Urbana: University of Illinois Press, 1985. Focuses on pamphlets and other writings discussing the place of women in society, with an emphasis on those by male authors.

Pearl Hogrefe, *Women of Action in Tudor England: Nine Biographical Sketches.* Ames: Iowa State University Press, 1977. Biographies of some of the well-known Englishwomen of this era.

Lynette Hunter and Sarah Hutton, eds., *Women, Science and Medicine, 1500–1700: Mothers and Sisters of the Royal Society.* Gloucestershire, UK: Sutton, 1997. Academic essays on women with some relationship to science (defined broadly to include household activities) in this era.

Margaret L. King, *Women of the Renaissance.* Chicago: University of Chicago Press, 1991. A detailed history of a range of different European women who filled many roles, from wife to nun to scholar.

Ulrike Klausmann, Marion Meinzerin, and Gabriel Kuhn, *Women Pirates and the Politics of the Jolly Roger.* Trans. Tyler Austin and Nicholas Levis. New York: Black Rose, 1997. Accounts of the lives and legends of women pirates across the centuries, drawing on popular sources and focusing on gender identity issues.

Patricia H. Labalme, ed., *Beyond Their Sex: Learned Women of the European Past.* New York: New York University Press, 1980. Essays on women scholars and writers including some from the Renaissance era.

Anny Latour, *The Borgias.* London: Elek, 1963. A history of this powerful Italian family, giving some information about some of the Borgia women.

Margaret MacCurtain and Mary O'Dowd, eds., *Women in Early Modern Ireland, 1500–1800.* Edinburgh: Edinburgh University Press, 1991. Academic essays on Irish women and their roles in a changing society. Includes Grace O'Malley.

Alan Macfarlane, *Marriage and Love in England: Modes of Reproduction, 1300–1840.* Oxford: Basil Blackwell, 1986. A social history of marriage customs and practices in England, focusing on men's decision-making processes.

Irene Mahoney, *Madame Catherine*. New York: Coward, McCann & Geoghegan, 1975. A biography of Catherine de Médicis, queen of France. Includes illustrations.

Roy T. Matthews and F. DeWitt Platt, *The Western Humanities*. Mountain View, CA: Mayfield, 1998. An overview of European culture with many illustrations and quotations from primary sources.

Garrett Mattingly, *Catherine of Aragon*. New York: Vintage, 1941. A biography of this Spanish queen of England focusing on her influence on the course of English history.

Sara Mendelson and Patricia Crawford, *Women in Early Modern England, 1550–1720*. Oxford: Oxford University Press, 1998. A detailed history of women's life cycles and women's relationships to the society in which they lived.

Marilyn Migiel and Juliana Schiesari, eds., *Refiguring Women: Perspectives on Gender and the Italian Renaissance*. Ithaca, NY: Cornell University Press, 1991. Academic articles focusing on gender issues.

Martha Moulsworth, *My Name Was Martha: A Renaissance Woman's Autobiographical Poem*. West Cornwall, CT: Locust Hill, 1993. One of the first autobiographies written in English. Includes extensive information on the historical background to this Renaissance wife's poem.

Wallace Notestein, *A History of Witchcraft in England from 1558 to 1718*. New York: Thomas Y. Crowell, 1968. Traces the English court cases related to witchcraft during the early modern era and offers an analysis of the rise and eventual decline of this legal, social, and religious movement.

Alison Plowden, *Tudor Women: Queens and Commoners*. New York: Atheneum, 1979. Focuses on the lives of Tudor queens from Elizabeth of York to Elizabeth I. Also describes the lives of average housewives of the period.

Mary Beth Rose, *Women in the Middle Ages and the Renaissance: Literary and Historical Perspectives*. Syracuse, NY: Syracuse University Press, 1986. Articles on a range of topics concerning women in society, including drama in Italian convents.

Nancy Rubin, *Isabella of Castile: The First Renaissance Queen*. New York: St. Martin's, 1991. Biography of an independent-minded woman. Records how she became queen, exerted power over rebellious nobles, supported Columbus's voyages, and initiated the Inquisition.

Louise Schleiner, *Tudor and Stuart Women Writers*. Bloomington: Indiana University Press, 1994. Discusses the work of a number of women writers, including Mary Herbert and Mary Wroth.

Simon Singh, *The Code Book: The Science of Secrecy from Ancient Egypt to Quantum Cryptography*. New York: Doubleday,

1999. An overview of encryption from the earliest times to the computer age. Includes a chapter on Mary Queen of Scots and her secret messages.

Jo Stanley, ed., *Bold in Her Breeches: Women Pirates Across the Ages.* San Francisco: Pandora, 1995. A summary of information on the topic, focused on cross-dressing and gender identity issues.

Frances Teague, *Bathsua Makin, Woman of Learning.* Lewisburg, PA: Bucknell University Press, 1998. A biography of a remarkable Englishwoman. Includes the text of her essay advocating women's education.

Betty Travitsky, ed., *The Paradise of Women: Writings by Englishwomen of the Renaissance.* Westport, CT: Greenwood, 1981. Examples of women's writing, organized by subject matter. Includes biographical information.

Gary Waller; *English Poetry of the Sixteenth Century.* New York, Longman, 1986. Useful discussion of the works of English Renaissance poets, including Mary Herbert and Mary Wroth.

Alison Weber, *Teresa of Avila and the Rhetoric of Femininity.* Princeton, NJ: Princeton University Press, 1990. An academic analysis of the writings of Teresa of Avila.

Alison Weir, *The Life of Elizabeth I.* New York: Ballantine, 1998. A detailed account of the life and long reign of the queen of England. Includes illustrations.

Merry E. Wiesner, *Women and Gender in Early Modern Europe.* 2nd ed. Cambridge: Cambridge University Press, 2000. A detailed history giving many individual portraits and information on a range of topics related to women's lives.

———, *Working Women in Renaissance Germany.* New Brunswick, NJ: Rutgers University Press, 1986. Has excellent detail on women's work according to the laws in six southern German cities.

Katharina M. Wilson, ed., *Women Writers of the Renaissance and Reformation.* Athens: University of Georgia Press, 1987. Essays on prominent women authors and their writing.

Joy Wiltenburg, *Disorderly Women and Female Power in the Street Literature of Early Modern England and Germany.* Charlottesville: University Press of Virginia, 1992. An analysis of women's roles based on the street ballads and broadsides published in England and Germany during the Renaissance.

Periodicals

Thomas G. Benedek, "The Changing Relationship Between Midwives and Physicians During the Renaissance," *Bulletin of the History of Medicine,* 1977.

Judith Brown and Jordan Goodman, "Women and Industry in Florence," *Journal of Economic History,* 1980.

Barton C. Hacker, "Women and Military Institutions in Early Modern Europe: A Reconnaissance," *Signs*, 1981.

Margaret Leah King, "Thwarted Ambitions: Six Learned Women of the Italian Renaissance," *Soundings* 1976.

E. William Monter, "Women in Calvinist Geneva," *Signs* 6, 1980.

Merry E. Wiesner, "Early Modern Midwifery: A Case Study," *International Journal of Women's Studies*, January/February 1983.

Diane Willen, "Women in the Public Sphere in Early Modern England: The Case of the Urban Working Poor," *Sixteenth Century Journal,* 1988.

Donald Woodward, "Wage Rates and Living Standards in Pre-Industrial England," *Past and Present*, May 1981.

Internet Sources

"Renaissance Women Online," http://textbase.wwp.brown.edu.

School of Mathematics and Statistics, University of St. Andrews, Scotland, "Pierre Gassendi," www-gap.dcs.st-and.ac.uk/~history/Mathematicians/Gassendi.html.

Frances Teague, "Bathsua Makin, Woman of Learning," www.pinn.net/~sunshine/book-sum/makin_b.html.

Hannah Wolley, "The Cooks Guide; or, Rare Receipts for Cookery," 1664, in "Renaissance Women Online," Women writers Project at Brown University, www.wwp.brown.edu/texts/textlist.author.html.

Index

Picture Credits

About the Authors

Ruth Dean is the president of The Writing Toolbox in Akron, Ohio. She researches and writes books, articles, Web site content, and corporate histories. She has taught English composition at the University of Akron.

Melissa Thomson has a doctorate in Renaissance English from Trinity College, Dublin. Thomson and Dean have written three other Lucent books, including *Women of the Middle Ages.*